HOW TO KILL A GOLDEN STATE

William Bronson

How to Kill a Golden State

Doubleday & Company, Inc., Garden City, New York
1968

By William Bronson

HOW TO KILL A GOLDEN STATE
STILL FLYING AND NAILED TO THE MAST
THE EARTH SHOOK, THE SKY BURNED

Portions of the chapters "Hard Sell in the Sky" and "The Giant Killers" appeared in *Cry California,* published by California Tomorrow, San Francisco, and are reprinted with permission of the publishers.

Contents

Acknowledgments

Most nonfiction books can only be done with the help of other knowledgeable and cooperative people. In the case of this book there were many others—some of whom must remain anonymous because of the nature of their employment and perhaps a few others because, in moving recently, my acknowledgement file went astray. With the hope that I have forgotten no one, I offer my warmest thanks:

To the indispensable photographers and photo sources listed in the back of the book.

To these individuals and organizations for their generous help of one kind or another: Rod Arkley, George Ballis, Ed Brady, Cheryl Brandt, Dave Brower, Bruce Brugmann, Mike Bry, Fran Colebird, Bob Cowgill, Ed Culin, Dick Dillon, Jackson Doyle, Don de la Peña, Ray Dunham, Joe Engbeck, Terry Feil, Wendy Koepel, Bob Golden, Sid Hammill, Martin Litton, Mike McCloskey, Pete McCloskey, Allan Ottley, Ron Partridge, Helen Reynolds, Malvina Reynolds, Harvey Richards, Gordon Robinson, Mel Scott, Ed Self, Frank Stead, Judy Tuttle, Don Vial, Jack Vietor, Milt Weiner, Joe Williamson, Leonard Wohletz, and Barry Wolman; the California Department of Parks and Recreation, Department of Public Health, Division of Highways, Office of the Corporation Commissioner, and Public Utilities Commission; the California Roadside Council, Foster & Kleiser, the Pacific Gas and Electric Company, *San Diego Magazine, San Francisco Magazine,* the San Francisco Planning Department, the Santa Clara County Planning Commission, the Save San Francisco Bay Association, the Save-the-Redwoods League and the Sierra Club.

To my patient and always encouraging editors at Doubleday, Elsa Anderson, and Luther Nichols (who thought up the idea of this book), and to Joseph Ascherl and Earl Tidwell for another fine job of design. The demanding job of shepherding the book, with all its bits and pieces, through production fell to Elsa Anderson, and so to her go my very special thanks.

To my confreres, Alf Heller and Sam Wood, president and executive director, respectively, of California Tomorrow, for the great body of source material they have developed in the past six years, and for their willing counsel and encouragement.

To Dick Reinhardt for his long and invaluable editorial labors at an early stage in the book's development. Without his help, I'm not sure I could have reduced the unmanageable ocean of data and ideas I had collected to the relatively rational order in which they now appear.

And last of all, to Marilyn, who endures me, and despite all the other demands on her time and energy gave her loving help in note taking, typing, editing, and critical commentary, although I must say I could do with a little less of the latter, generally speaking.

For my children,
Knox, Meg, Nate and Benjy

Introduction

IN 1963 a book called *Beautiful California* was published by the company that publishes *Sunset*, The Magazine of Western Living. It is largely the work of my good friend, Paul C. Johnson, under whose direction at *Sunset* in 1956 and 1957 I learned much of what I know about putting books together. *Beautiful California* is a book of considerable quality—the binding, the paper, the printing, the commentary, the layouts, etc. The photography includes some of the outstanding work of California's best photographers.

The book was a genuine best-seller. Governor Brown gave a copy to the Pope. Many reviewers praised it, and it deservedly won a prize for the care with which it was designed. Its only fault lies in the fact that while it appears to be a work of non-fiction, it is not.

The jacket copy reads, "Here for the first time is the *complete picture of California,* presenting in outstanding photographs the many varied faces of the state." In truth, one face is missing, and that is the California where most of us work, sleep, travel, play, breathe and dream. This California is a hell of a mess and getting worse. We live in Ugly California. And despite the valiant struggling by those who know and care about what is happening, the ugliness grows at a rate that outraces all our present efforts to control it. The dimensions of ugliness are varied and often overlap: freeways/autos/smog/urban sprawl/strip development/*ad nauseum*—pollution—destruction of wildlife—dreariness of landscape and small towns—ugly social sores—filthy streets—cheap-jack architecture, and more.

In the old days we had such abundant land and the land was so rich that waste didn't seem to matter. But millions of acres of our prime agricultural land has fallen to the tract builders and much more is doomed. Litter, endless billboards, honkytonk commercialism, and banal slurb construction line the highways. Poisons and sewage pollute our bays, lakes and rivers. Smog chokes Los Angeles, but what the San Francisco Bay Area and the Central Valley can anticipate will make Los Angeles seem desirable. And this is but part of the story.

When I was born in 1926 there were slightly less than five million people in California, a large number of whom were immigrants, as opposed to us elite native-born. Today we are at the twenty million mark. We were handed a tradition of easy-going life which rested largely upon two natural factors —good weather and seemingly unlimited land, air and water resources. These are the features that attracted my grandparents, and to a lesser degree, attract today's out-of-staters.

California's population has doubled every twenty years, give or take one or two, ever since statehood was granted in 1850. And in this fact lies the understanding of what we witness today. The ruination of California is the result of population impact on limited resources of land, air and water in the absence of adequate public policy, planning and controls.

Our problems can be found elsewhere in varying degrees, so why pick on California? Mainly because California has led the rest of the world into the age of mass affluence and has become standing testimony to man's infinite capacity to befoul and destroy in the quest for an ever-higher standard of living. I think I speak for the great majority when I question the value of more and more goods if those goods are gained only at the price of clean air, sweet water, songbirds, uncluttered skylines, shaded streets, unspoiled landscape, and indeed our very health.

And so I have attempted to put "the mess" into some kind of intelligible order; to distinguish between pollution, which is reversible, and destruction, which is not; to point out some of the causes, direct and indirect; to suggest solutions; and to put the finger on some of those who profit by postponing the bold steps we must take if we are to restore, at least partially, the sublime qualities which once made California a magic word around the world. Nothing is impossible; if we can go to the moon, we can recreate a decent environment.

In gathering material for other books and articles, I've always reached a point of diminishing returns before taking up the painful job of committing ideas to paper. With this book, the reverse has been true. When I began work on the project in fall of 1963, I expected to complete it in the following spring. I didn't know it then, but I had opened Pandora's box.

The book is a collection of glimpses into the box. It is an illustrated collection of fact, comment, and judgment on the state of physical resources and quality of life in California. Yet it is but a sampling. With perhaps one or two exceptions, the subject of every chapter could be (or already has been) extended into book length—and even that result would remain but a beginning of full description and understanding of the problems considered herein.

During the three years I have worked intermittently on this project, many books touching in one degree or another on the subject of my own work have been published: Peter Blake's *God's Own Junkyard;* Stuart Udall's *Quiet Crisis;* Mel Scott's *The Future of San Francisco Bay;* Ray Dasmann's *The Destruction of California;* Philip Hyde and François Leydet's *The Last Redwoods* (one of many splendid Sierra Club publications); Samuel Wood and Alfred Heller's *California Going, Going . . .* and *The Phantom Cities of California;* Samuel Wood and Daryl Lembke's *The Federal Threats to the California Landscape* are among the prominent ones that come to mind. Rachael Carson's *Silent Spring,* of course, stands as the masterpiece in all the literature that deals with man's well-meaning attempts to destroy the ecology and wreck the earth. Yet with all that has been written, the California public has but a glimmer of understanding of the enormity of the problems it faces.

Admittedly, there are other problems that make those covered in this book fade into insignificance—Vietnam, the proliferation of nuclear weapons, the world population explosion, the struggle for social and economic justice in our country—to name the more obvious.

But I can't make over the world. Indeed it is presumptuous to think that this book will accomplish much along the lines it is intended. Someone asked Ammon Henacy, the pacifist and Catholic anarchist, in reference to his lifetime of antiwar activity, whether it wouldn't be better to light one candle than to curse the darkness. He replied that you had to do both. And that is what I have attempted to do here: to raise hell with the wreckers and to suggest some measures we must take if and when we decide that the good life is something more than that which comes in a package from the supermarket.

Despite the awesome political power of those who make money in the process of polluting and destroying the resources of California, we have it within our power to halt the spread of blight and to return this bright land to the splendor it once was. Right now, today, we have the constitutional right, the technology and the money. The problem is how to muster them.

It isn't going to be easy. The opposition is formidable and, within the constraints of the law, ruthless. Our era may well be remembered as the Age of Paid Liars. That's a harsh way of putting it, but it is my studied opinion that never before has such a premium been put on outright falsehood in the conduct of man's affairs. Private interests use lying to a greater extent than government, but both are culpable.

The liars are, I presume, otherwise honorable men, but when it comes to protecting their own, be it the right to destroy the last redwoods, for instance, or muck up the waters and the air, cover the cities and roadsides with billboards, ram a freeway through a park, build an instant slum, dam the last wild rivers, or wipe out other creatures with whom we share the earth, they use the outright lie as freely as if it were sanctioned by Heaven.

This is one reason I have leaned so heavily upon photo documentation. One may argue with my words all day and night, but the truths the pictures show can't be denied.

Although I may have generated a few original ideas in the process of doing this book, and perhaps new ways to expose older ideas, *How to Kill a Golden State* remains largely a distillation and synthesis of the work of other people, almost all of whom are Californians.

I can't emphasize enough the tremendous good that has been done by that relative handful of people who have and are working furiously to save California from itself. Most of them are concerned with only parts of our chamber of horrors. They are motivated by a variety of drives—love of beauty, love of justice, compassion, nostalgia, professional ambition, love of battle, and more. Their personal politics range all over the political spectrum. All are concerned with saving, maintaining or upgrading the enviroment. Most of them speak in behalf of coming generations, and in so doing meet that basic moral responsibility ignored by too many who should know better. They constantly challenge our current hierarchy of values. They believe in the sanctity of life and the possibility of perfectibility of man, or if not the latter, at least the preservation of man until that noble notion has had a chance to be tested.

At any rate, it's my hope that this book will prove to be a cudgel they can use. It is, after all, a tract formed on their work.

WILLIAM BRONSON

Berkeley
October 1967

Soot and Corruption

Two views of San Francisco looking west from the same vantage point in Berkeley's Claremont District hills. The smoggy scene, right, was shot directly into the sun on an autumn afternoon in 1964. The clear day, above, was the rule until ten or twelve years ago; today it is the brown pall. The San Francisco Bay airshed is potentially a worse smog trap than the Los Angeles basin.

IF it were not for the fact that California's smog problem could become—if it isn't already—a man-killing tragedy, I might take provincial pleasure in pointing out one of the great ironies in California history. We northern Californians have long told of the many early migrants to Los Angeles who came on the advice of their physicians in the hope that the warm, dry climate would cure them of a variety of respiratory ailments. "Lungers," as they were called, flocked to the glorious Los Angeles basin, and a new kind of American city grew. Today, a doctor who sent a patient with emphysema, bronchitis, or asthma to Los Angeles for a cure would have his license taken from him.

Angelenos of my generation can remember the sweet perfume from the orange groves and the sight of sparkling snow-capped mountains in the distance. The perfume, with the orange groves, has now all but vanished and the mountains lie, almost always, behind a veil of brown smog. Progress has taken its toll. This unique by-product of growth and affluence caught up with Los Angeles in the early years of World War II, and as a result the town has enjoyed the biggest, longest-lived embarrassment in the history of civic press-agentry.

It is not my intention to descend into a traditional Northern California attack on the excesses and shortcomings of Los Angeles. It's an old game and it used to be fun. As I wrote the first draft of this chapter, my throat was irritated and my eyes were watery and reddened, thanks not to the evening before, but to a routine San Francisco Bay Area smog attack—the fourteenth of that particular month. We once snickered at the plight of Los Angeles, but now the joke is on us all. The word smog is no longer funny *anywhere* in California.

The Bay Area may still be a few years behind Los Angeles in the matter of smog affliction, but in this and other areas of environmental concern the gap is closing. Whether we like it or not, the Losangelesation of the California lowlands, coastlands and part of the mountain and desert lands is in process.

Air pollution is anything but new. Industrial cities of the East and Middle West lived with serious pollution resulting from the uncontrolled burning of coal and fuel oil for decades before the public demanded correction. As a result of public demand, the air over such cities as Pittsburgh and Saint Louis is markedly cleaner than that over Los Angeles. The problem in London, where the word smog is believed to have originated, reached a climax in 1952 when deaths during a sulfurous sky-darkening, choking smog attack rose from the weekly average of two thousand to *five* thousand. A smog attack in Donora, Pennsylvania, in 1948 is credited with killing twenty persons and injuring five thousand more. Those who didn't die during the attack, have suffered much higher death and illness rates than fellow townsmen who were not stricken at the time.

But on the Pacific coast the offshore breezes kept the air clear and pure until one otherwise normal wartime day in Los Angeles the newspapers reported what they called "daylight dimout." It was on September 8, 1943, that smog, Los Angeles smog as we know it today, made its first appearance. One of the newspapers reported, "Thousands of eyes smarted. Many wept, sneezed and coughed. Throughout the downtown area and into the hills the fumes spread their irritation." Today this language would be laughed at. Smog conditions are reported regularly and dispassionately with the other weather data. Smog is a climatological element as real as sunshine or rain.

There are all kinds of air pollution and air pollutants. Some are exotic California specialties such as peat dust from the asparagus fields of the Sacramento River Delta or particles of dried turkey droppings that are picked up by winds during the dry season in the San Joaquin Valley. We have ample quantities of the oxides of sulfur, which in solution form sulfurous and sulfuric acids. (These come largely from the burning of fuel oil.) Fly ash, metal particles, hydrogen sulfide, carbon monoxide, and a wide variety of other gases, solid particles, and aerosols can be found in our air. But it is the production of what is called "photochemical" smog that now most seriously concerns California.

I can recall my fascination with the amount of soot that collected on window sills and porch rails in industrial New Jersey when I worked there briefly in 1946. I was fresh from California and had never seen anything like it. Today the amount of grimy fallout in Berkeley is at times just as bad as anything I saw in Bayonne or Hoboken. If our problem were only dirt, annoying as it is, we might be willing to live with it. But photochemical smog is much more than mere soot and is as potentially dangerous as the sulfur dioxide laden smogs of London and the eastern American industrial regions.

The easiest way to understand California's smog is to consider the areas affected as great mixing bowls. The San Francisco Bay Region and the Central Valley are almost literally that, while the Los Angeles basin lacks only a mountain barrier on the coastside. Toward California from deep in the Pacific Ocean hot air masses move slowly and steadily. As the air approaches the coast, the lowest layer in the mass is cooled by cold Pacific coast currents. This cooler layer of air, being denser than the warm air above, cannot rise. The layer of warmer air acts literally as a lid to the mixing bowl. Normally, the temperature drops as altitude increases, but this inversion is characteristic of California weather, particularly in the late summer and fall.

Into the great mixing bowl, then, add millions of people and automobiles, factories, trash burners, etc., and set them all to work. This alone is not enough to cause a smog attack. That comes when the inversion layer is lower than the surrounding mountains, when the winds are very gentle or absent entirely, and when the ultraviolet rays from the sun have had an hour or two to work on the raw materials poured into the air by the millions of people as they go about the business of the day.

While some of the raw materials of California smog are deadly all by themselves, the worst irritants are produced by chemical reaction between certain hydrocarbons which enter the air largely as a result of the operation of automobiles, and nitrogen oxide which is produced in virtually any kind of burning.

The resulting compounds are called photochemical smog, which consists principally of ozone, a couple of aldehydes, ketones, poorly understood particulates which require SO_2 to form PAN (peroxyacetyl nitrate), and nitrogen dioxide. These substances, together or singly, make the eyes water, irritate the respiratory system, crack rubber tires, stunt and kill plants, depress the spirit, and darken the skies. If these were not enough, carbon monoxide levels also build up during a smog attack.

We do not know how much smog costs us in dollars each year. The U. S. Public Health Service estimates that the figure is on the order of $65 per person per year in the United States—cleaning bills, laundry, ruined paint, destruction of metal and stone building materials, etc. But who has computed the cost in absenteeism? Who can put a price on the psychological depression that accompanies a sharp smog attack? How much do the farmers lose each year in plant and animal damage?

Even if we could add up the cost in all these elusive categories, who among us would be wise enough to estimate the value of the extra twenty or so years of life that every other lung-cancer victim might have expected to enjoy had he not spent the better part of his years breathing smog. Ask the wife of the man who is dying of emphysema how much the years he might have had are worth to her. Admittedly, there is no "scientific" proof that garden-variety smog shortens the lives of those who must live in it. To claim otherwise would be to misuse the term "scientific proof." But must we wait for incontrovertible proof before we are willing to spend the money required to clean up the air? Dr. H. E. Landsberg, a biometorologist with the U. S. Department of Commerce Weather Bureau, speaking in September of 1964, summed up the prospect if extraordinary steps are not taken now to control air pollution. "The population," he said, "will be an allergic lot, with subacute carbon monoxide poisoning and lead poisoning, suffering from chronic bronchitis and emphysema, and dying from sulfur-dioxide-induced cardiorespiratory insufficiency or from benz-pyrene-stimulated lung cancer."

We haven't, of course, been standing idly by. Hundreds of millions of dollars have been spent on devices and procedures that will reduce the amount of potential pollutant in the air. In 1957, for instance, the Los Angeles Air Pollution Control Board banned burning in backyard incinerators. The million and a half incinerators were worth something like $40 million. The public reaction was hostile because it didn't end the smog problem, but the ban did stop a daily emission from this source of 600 tons of formaldehydes, aldehydes and other polluting gases and particles. The saving amounts to more than a pound a week for each person in the Los Angeles basin.

By 1962 about $100,000,000 had been spent on some 9000 factory control devices in Los Angeles County. Without them, Los Angeles air would be laden with an additional 4600 tons of sulfur dioxide and other pollutants per day.

These heroic measures have lowered the number of Los Angeles smog alerts in the last ten years, but it is just a matter of time before smog levels will, because of sheer growth in the number of automobiles on the road, surpass the old marks. As D. J. Callaghan, the Bay Area Air Pollution Control District Chief Administrative Officer, said of San Francisco Bay, "Our fight is a losing one." Between 1956 and 1964, the amount of photochemical smog doubled, despite efforts that had removed about 800 tons of pollutant which otherwise would have entered the atmosphere each day.

No one knows for certain what percent of the polluting products of combustion are attributable to motor vehicles in relation to other sources. But according to the Statistical Abstract of the United States, 1963, the total available horsepower of the country's autos, buses and motorcycles is twenty times as great as the horsepower available in all other engines or turbines which convert fuels and forces (wind and water) in all our factories, mines, electrical generating plants

(hydro, steam and nuclear), aircraft, ships, railroads and farms.

It is not to excuse industry from strict air-pollution control to say that the internal combustion engine is clearly the villain of the piece, and we have tried to act on this knowledge. Since 1959, we have maintained faith in the idea that state-required crankcase and exhaust emission control devices would prove to be the solution. The history of legislation in this field is largely a matter of prolonged resistance by Detroit and flip-flops by the California legislature in response to shifts in the nature of public outcry.

Perhaps the program will work as intended, and for the sake of argument, let's assume that the control devices will work as well as they are supposed to. If they do, eighty percent of the emissions of unburned and partially burned hydrocarbons and carbon monoxide will be eliminated.

What will we have gained? Dr. Phillip Leighton, one of the world's leading photochemists, has shown that in 1985, even with eighty percent emission control, smog levels will equal the dangerously high levels of 1955. But even if *all* hydrocarbon and carbon monoxide emissions are eliminated, the prospect remains bleak. For to date, we have established no law to control the levels of nitrogen dioxide, a killer in its own right.

The prospect of ever-increasing nitrogen dioxide levels is potentially a far greater health hazard than anything we have yet witnessed. The prospect is so frightening that experts such as Dr. Leighton and chemist Donald E. Carr, whose book *The Breath of Life* deals with the air-pollution problem in depth, find the prospect of *failure* of the emission control device program in California to be desirable. It now appears that it may be better to continue to pour hydrocarbons into the air to combine with nitrogen dioxide in production of photochemical smog than to allow nitrogen dioxide concentrations to increase.

There appears to be but one answer. As our numbers continue to grow, we will simply have to give up much of the open burning of petroleum products, and this means finding a replacement for the internal combustion engine as motive power for ground transportation.

Most experts, if not all, agree to this conclusion, and they also generally agree that the likeliest alternative is electric power, probably in the form of the high-energy fuel cell.

It is undoubtedly true that the political power of the oil and auto industries is at this time sufficient to block legislation that would lead to such a changeover. Granting this, then, it would appear incumbent upon state and federal governments to develop programs in which both Detroit and the petroleum industries could participate, profitably, from the outset in development of vehicles driven by non-polluting engines. The high-energy fuel cell, if that is to be the energy source, does not generate power out of thin air. Power-generating plants operated by the oil companies can be built to burn the petrochemical fuels in non-polluting closed systems to charge the cells, and each company's network of gas stations could market them. The automobile industry, which will continue to build vehicles for ground transportation regardless of motive power, must be similarly induced to partici-

pate in the conversion process. I do not know how best to bring this about, but I know it can and must be done. It will be expensive, but we can afford it.

The American motoring public buys something in excess of seventy billion gallons of gasoline a year, and of this incredible amount, ten percent comes out the exhaust pipe unburned. This means we are wasting considerably in excess of $2 billion worth of fuel each year. Some say that pollution control is too expensive and that the public will not stand for it. The truth is that pollution is too expensive—in lives, in property loss, in daily enjoyment and if nothing else, in gasoline.

Having thought long and hard on this subject, I have come to believe that it will take a massive human kill directly attributable to air pollution before we embark, for the sake of our children if not ourselves, on the heroic program necessary to restore the air to the healthful, comfortable levels that we once enjoyed. We don't *have* to let it happen, but in light of the faint-hearted way we've toyed with the problem to date, it takes little courage to say that happen it will.

Although the automobile is everyone's favorite culprit in the smog wars, industry of all kinds must share in the blame. This shot was taken in San Francisco near the San Mateo county line. Although two of the Bay Area's four open-hearth steel mills shut down operations rather than meet the Air Pollution Control District's emission standards, many other less obvious targets for control continue to sully the air.

The view of Los Angeles Civic Center beyond Chinatown. This classic series has been published many times but it tells the story well. After more than twenty years, smog still makes front-page headlines when the going, all too often, gets rough.

University of California at Berkeley in the foreground, with Mount Tamalpais in the distance. Picture taken after an autumn rain in 1964.

The UC campus seen from the same spot in the Berkeley hills during a sickening three-day smog attack in late October, 1964.

The snow-capped San Gabriel Mountains as they looked at the turn of the century.

Today, the smog may obscure the mountains for months on end.

Even Eureka, on the north coast in the heart of the redwood logging country, has an air-pollution problem, and with the recently constructed pulp mill to the windward of town the problem could become worse.

The U. S. Navy, in arrogant disregard for the open burning ban imposed by the Air Pollution Control District, regularly befouls the air with its fire-control drills at Treasure Island. The drills are undoubtedly valuable, but San Francisco Bay isn't the place for them.

Smoggy San Francisco from Twin Peaks, looking east to the Oakland/Berkeley hills.

Los Angeles, of course.

These four big fellows, hauling tomatoes and belching forth illegal black plumes, are part of the growing diesel fleet which is yet to feel the hand of the air-pollution control officer. Emission control for diesels is overdue.

Someone once suggested that for every child born a tree be planted; for every automobile sold, a thousand, and for every jet airliner built, a hundred thousand.

The diesel engine may not, as some studies show, contribute significantly to photochemical smog, but it can and does spew forth prodigious amounts of particulate matter which begrimes the scene. We have anti-black-plume laws, but they are difficult to enforce. A properly tuned and maintained diesel will burn cleanly, but it's cheaper to break the law.

The freeway now bypasses this stretch between Oceanside and Carlsbad, but for years travelers were treated to the quaint sight of the city of Carlsbad dumping its filthy sewage outfall into the Buena Vista Lagoon Wild Life Sanctuary, which is shown in the views on this page. The stench was awful. In 1965, five years after the project was initiated, the Carlsbad—Buena Vista joint sewage system was opened. To mark the occasion, local officials removed clothespins from their noses at the dedication ceremonies.

A Richmond chemical
factory is one of many
San Francisco Bay
Area industries which have
over the years deliberately
or by accident added
injurious wastes to the
waters of the Bay.

The City of San Francisco has always been
a significant polluter of bay waters. This is
Aquatic Park, site of the San Francisco Maritime Museum and the San Franciso Maritime
State Historical Monument. Notice the water
lovers who, obviously, don't bother to read
the signs.

According to water pollution control officials the cities and counties are less co-operative, in general, than industry in complying with pollution standards. Although these particular instances may by now have been cleaned up, sewage contamination of recreational resources remains a statewide problem.

In the 1870s or 1880s, photographer O. V. Lange of Berkeley wrote these captions for his pictures: Above, "Near view of a lumber mill in Pescadero Basin near La Honda, San Mateo Co. Showing the dumping of sawdust into the creek, thereby polluting the stream and killing all fish." Left, "A lumber mill in Pescadero Basin, San Mateo Co., just over the divide north of Big Basin Park, in Santa Cruz Co. This scene is an effective object lesson and typical of many others. The mountain side cut away, then washed bare, the creeks choked with debris, its soil burned hard, and every vestige of humus and forest-sponge is gone."

And the destruction of our stream beds by the loggers has continued unabated to this day. Here the operators have destroyed salmon and steelhead spawning grounds on the South fork of the Gualala River in Mendocino County.

This logging road, because it was not built to avoid erosion, clearly violates the State Forestry Practices Act. The Act is a set of rules designed by the logging industry which, even if it were enforced (and it is not), would be inadequate to protect our timber resource, our wildlife and our watersheds. The act is a cheap and cynical farce, and everyone close to the problem knows it.

A silt-laden Sierra stream, once a trout-spawning bed, wrecked in defiance of the law by loggers. The California logging conspiracy—that lying, evasive, double-talking alliance of lumber producers—will cost us dearly for centuries to come. Essentially exploitive in nature, the loggers exact a tribute from the land, in terms of wilderness, wildlife, soil, recreational potential, productivity and the like, alongside which Cosa Nostra operations appear sickly and insignificant. We desperately need wholesale revision and massive stiffening in the laws that govern the use of our dwindling timber resource.

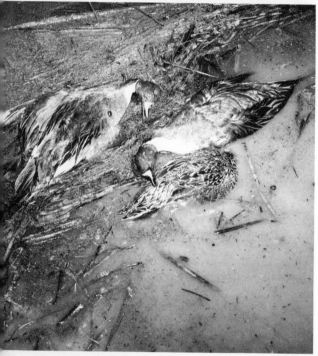

The dreadful tale of the effects of widespread use of biocides in our time was brilliantly put down by Rachel Carson in *Silent Spring:* it is a story too complicated to digest in these pages. California is the country's leading agricultural state and as such is the greatest consumer of poisons. The wildlife kill is disturbing, not only in its own right, but for what it portends. The massive impregnation of soil and waters that these kills make manifest can, if unchecked, lead to such a disruption of the ecology that agriculture itself may be severely damaged. The poisons don't discriminate between friendly and unfriendly organisms. All three of these scenes were shot in the sloughs of the Sacramento Valley. We have failed to direct our pest-control research efforts along natural biological lines in favor of chemical controls, and this is due, sad to relate, to the oil and chemical companies who do the research or subsidize it. These enterprises are, whether we like it or not, in the business of making money by tampering with the ecology and not in the business of preserving the earth and the life upon it.

Although poisoning of agricultural workers is an annual scandal, the press makes little news of it. After all, these people are very unimportant, and one shouldn't rock the $3.8 billion agri-business. The shocking fact is that *all* of us now carry in our systems more pesticide residue than is allowed in beef carcasses shipped interstate. Only in 1966 were federal studies undertaken to detect the effects of poisons on agricultural workers, our latter-day slaves. California's century-old farm-labor scandal is getting a better airing these days. Hopefully, the shameful *bracero* program appears to be dead, despite anguished cries from the big growers and their sycophants, a noisy bunch that includes California's actor-politicians, George Murphy and Ronald Reagan.

San Francisco Assemblyman Charles Myers surveys the Brisbane dumpsite for San Francisco's garbage. Dumps are only one source of the ever-growing stench in our air. And although stench alone is not a significant pollution concern, it is increasing. Other sources: sewage treatment plants, pulp mills, the internal combustion engine, refineries. The worst stink-producers in my experience are the Sonoma County applesauce packing houses, whose openly dumped wastes combine the worst olfactory elements of raw sewage and well-aged garbage.

Unlike stench, noise is an ever-growing menace to physical and mental health. Without question, the inadequately muffled diesel engine is the worst offender in this sector, and as our freeway system spreads, so will the number of these rubber-tired freight cars increase. One of the worst errors the Division of Highways has made is its abject failure to engineer against ear pollution. Even if we should get really effective muffler-control legislation, the scream of the big-rig tires against the freeway pavement will remain a sleep destroyer.

Hard Sell in the Sky

No people in the world are hounded so relentlessly by outdoor advertising as the California public. Is there another state in the nation, or for that matter another nation, that even approaches California in the quantity, vulgarity and chaos of visual huckstering? The mess, above right, could be anywhere in any of our larger cities. The nearest thing to it, in my experience, is San Diego—a town which otherwise has much to commend it—but if you'll look carefully, you'll see downtown Oakland in the distance. The beauty of San Francisco's city hall, below right, is mocked and diminished by useless billboards. Like a pack of scurvy jackals, billboards prey on any and all who pass their way. Only the blind are spared. The neon sign, as exemplified on the left, is, whether we like it or not, a unique American art form, and like other hard-sell elements of our culture, it bespeaks something less than sublime.

HARD sell visual pollution is one of the most easily corrected forms of environmental plague that we endure. Compared to the problem of smog, say, this one is so simple to solve it is a wonder we put up with it at all.

By "hard sell" I mean outdoor advertising that wrecks our skylines—billboards and on-premise commercial sign excesses. Perhaps the explanation for our tolerance is that we accept as truth the idea that you can't fight city hall and can't interfere with someone else's so-called "property rights," even if it happens that he is interfering with other's rights.

For there should be no question about it —the outdoor advertising that now flourishes in California *does* intrude on our rights. It trespasses on our privacy and violates our personal right to go about the land without being nagged perpetually to buy, *buy,* BUY! It is intrusive and invasive. It imposes upon us not because we *invite* it as we do when we buy a newspaper or magazine or turn on a radio or TV set, but merely because in the course of a walk or drive along our publicly-owned streets and highways, we cannot avoid seeing it.

Almost every other form of advertising can be ignored, turned off, rejected. All but outdoor advertising. The industry points out in one of its propaganda pamphlets that outdoor advertising has gone on since the time of the cave men. Primitive man, they say, "communicated" out of doors by drawing sublime pictures of bison and musk oxen on the walls of caves. As if man's first great art is somehow related to their shrieking commercialism. Further, they state, "there are two kinds of advertising—indoor (newspapers, magazines, junk mail, radio and TV) and outdoor. They thus imply that since two kinds exist, both thereby somehow have an unquestioned right to exist.

Although billboard interests harp, to the point of desperation, on their contention that outdoor advertising is a necessary part of "free choice," billboards have practically nothing to do with free choice. As a matter of fact, advertising in general has tended to standardize goods to such an extent that there is very little choice among mass-pro-

This sign can be read by anyone with near-normal vision from anywhere in line of sight within the city of San Francisco or the Bay Bridge—a distance up to four miles. There is no truth to the old story, as far as I can find out, that the dental associations subsidize soft-drink advertising, but think of the business this monster has generated for dentists over the years.

duced products, either in quality or price.

But let's assume that advertising is beneficial, indeed, essential to our economy. Even granting this, the billboard business could be completely eliminated and the economy would not be affected. Billboard advertising does not create true demand for goods, because the type of advertising that can be done on a high speed road is limited to name identification and product "image." ("Because outdoor advertising speaks to a market on the move, it must speak quickly, memorably, attractively and repeatedly. . . .")

The extreme example of this fact is gasoline advertising. No gasoline advertising of any sort actually sells gasoline, with the possible exception of a few activities in the field of travel promotion. People don't drive more as a result of gasoline advertising. Gasoline advertising—a lot of it in billboards—is not a stimulant to demand, but an intra-mural struggle among gasoline producers to gain a larger share of the market.

In any case, the advertising function can be performed adequately by other media, all of which (with a couple of exceptions, such as junk mail and telephone solicitation) provide a service of some sort for their intrusion on the customer.

The billboard business argues that it "serves the consumer by guiding him to the place where he can satisfy his needs"—meaning, it gives information on food, lodgings, etc. Thus, it presumes to provide an indispensable service to the traveler.

In actual fact, however, billboards provide information solely about places that have the money and inclination to pay for highway advertising. The truth is, you can't get from billboards the sort of information you really need as a traveler—the kind you get out of an auto club travel book, or even out of the phone book. If a person needs this kind of information, there are certainly more convenient, simple, accurate, informative ways to get it than by reading highway billboards.

For example, any city or town could set up turn-out areas along its approaches where it could provide poster-sized space for pure advertising, and with the ads, a business directory of the kinds of services a traveler might be looking for—everything from garages to short-order restaurants. For the billboard business to try to justify its existence on this score is an indication of the bankruptcy of its claim to legitimacy.

To those of us who are concerned about esthetics, the case against billboards—or, at least, the case for limiting the size and location of billboards and commercial signs—seems obvious. Yet, we have very spotty public action against offensive billboards, President Johnson's highway beautification program to the contrary notwithstanding. The new Federal legislation does not *eliminate* billboards; it merely sets some of them further back from the road, and with the probable result that we'll just get *bigger* signs set behind the 660-foot limit.

Why? Part of the reason is certainly the political and economic power of the billboard users. In addition, about a quarter of a million property owners in the United States get income by renting land for billboards. In California the number of rural signs doubled between 1950 and 1960, according to a report in the *Reader's Digest*. Even with this great increase in space, the demand outstrips the supply. And the increase in urban billboard is even more formidable. It will be in the cities that the last billboard wars are fought.

To the landlord who owns a building with a billboard on the roof, to a farmer who makes a hundred dollars a year by leasing ground for a signboard, the esthetic factor seems trivial. Jobs are, in truth, created by the billboard business; and, God knows, there is money in it. These economic and political factors have all but overwhelmed the well-intentioned citizens who would like to get rid of billboards on esthetic grounds alone.

But it may not be necessary, indeed it may not be wise, to base the anti-billboard attack on esthetic grounds. Howard Gossage, head of an advertising agency in San Francisco, is the first writer (and the only one, as far as I know) to take the position that billboards will never be proscribed on esthetic grounds, for, in the long run, this raises an irresolvable question, a matter of taste: Are billboards pretty, or aren't they? If you argue on pure esthetics, you're going to lose.

Gossage's alternative argument is this: "Outdoor advertising is peddling a commodity it does not own, and without the owner's permission: your field of vision." In other words, your line of sight belongs to you, and no commercial intrusions on it should be allowed.

Billboards, he reasons, are differentiated from other uninvited objects that might pass your eye in that they have no other purpose or function than to do this—to trespass. Nations are hotly protective of their air space, Gossage notes. Yet the air space of individuals is "intentionally violated by billboards every day of the year."

We can't control the visual pollution of other states, but should we have to suffer the mutely shouting invasion of the outdoor advertisers until the federal government moves in to save us, which may be never? Hawaii has no billboards, but can anyone suggest that life is poorer in Hawaii than it is in California?

The first thing we can do is create a statewide moratorium on further billboard construction. This form of prevention would not cost anything, except perhaps in unrealized hopes for the industry. I am sure there are exceptions to a *total* ban that should be considered, but they should be few and far between.

As for phasing out existing rural billboards, this can be done under such legislation as Title I of the Highway Beautification Act. The great fault with this law when passed in 1965 was the provision for compensation to billboard companies for removal of their signs. This provision was a great victory for the industry and it must be removed if the law is to be effective.

The next big step in blight control—elimination of urban billboards—will be difficult to enact into law but the need is clearly evident. There is no more justification for the use of city streets and urban highways for billboards than rural highways. The courts have already ruled that billboards anywhere are "nuisances" whose "sole value consists of being viewed from public ways," and that they may be abated by public action. It will be under this logic that the final battle against billboards in our cities will be waged.

The ubiquitous flickering Nervous Sign pictured here has added a new dimension to California's night-time visual pollution. No photograph or series of photographs can quite capture both the intrusive brilliance and the visual titubation of the Nervous Sign, but here is one in six of its phases. The sign flashes through this series in approximately one second.

The evil days on which on-premise outdoor advertising has fallen is no better indicated than by the story of that which I prefer to call the Nervous Sign.

Anyone with 20/400 vision or better who has driven along a few of California's thousands and thousands of miles of cheap commercial strip development is familiar with the Nervous Sign. It is everywhere. Its forms are few, but its numbers are many. And each one beckons with a syncopated visual shriek that cannot be ignored. The Nervous Sign is a vulgar tic on the face of California's small business life, and like other excesses in the jungle world of outdoor advertising, it is ultimately self-defeating.

The Nervous Sign carries no message. It is designed for one purpose, to attract the eye of the motorist to *another* sign. In the words of one proud manufacturer:

"The unique lighting action of the Superior Animator attracts the conscious and unconscious eye. Its unusual action compels people to look at your sign from three to five times as they approach. From a great distance it appears to be moving at one speed—as you approach, the speed appears to change—the closer you come the more rapid its change. The action borders on the verge of hypnosis.

"The Animator with its Unique Design, Fast Action, Bright Color and Intense Brilliance compels people to look at your sign and place of business whether they want to or not . . .

"Its design delivers a message—'read this sign!' 'this is the place!' 'stop here!' 'buy here!'

"Survey tests have proven that there is nothing more penetrating to the human memory than the design of the Animator. It stays with everyone and is never forgotten."

They do not mention that the Nervous Sign is, at least to the moderately sensitive onlooker, about as comfortable as a wart under the eyelid.

Although the sign's mechanisms are guaranteed (one manufacturer gives two years), the light bulbs are not and for good reason. Bulb life is affected not only by normal voltage fluctuation, but by the amount of vibration the filaments are subjected to, and the average Nervous Sign is exposed to much—gusty winds, passing trucks, and slammed doors all hasten filament failure. It is rare to find a fully functioning Nervous Sign.

As the novelty wears off and the bulbs begin to go, the owners either don't have replacements on hand, or they don't have the time and money to bother with it, or they just don't care. And the sign becomes shabby and offensive for its shabbiness, just as it offended with its vulgar intrusiveness when new.

A fully functioning Nervous Sign works with the compelling brilliance of an arc welder, but when it fades it has no more appeal than a broken toy or a cigarette butt.

Perhaps the ancient doctrine of *caveat emptor* is sufficient to protect small businessmen who are prospects for the Nervous Sign. Many who have purchased them say they are satisfied and pleased, at least in the first month or so after installation. Regardless, the buyer-beware approach will contribute no more to the beautification of our streets than would an appeal to the sign makers and merchants to exercise the virtues of moderation and good taste.

The Nervous Sign is, of course, merely a symptom, not a disease in itself. It is the natural outgrowth of the slurbanization of California. Strip development, stupidly allowed to spread like wild morning glory from our urban centers, is utterly dependent on the motoring shopper—be it in San Bernardino or San Jose.

To compete for the passing eye, signs along the strips were made bigger, more exaggerated, more vulgar; flags and spinning plastic discs were draped from poles and rooftops; where one sign had once been sufficient, three or six had to be added.

Then into this visual chaos came the Nervous Sign, so brilliant and irritating that wherever it was placed it stuck out like a sore thumb. But this was only the beginning of another cycle, a cycle that has not yet reached its conclusion.

For while one Nervous Sign per mile may work to good effect for its owner, that effect is completely lost when the neighbors begin putting them up. And that is where we are today. We have chaos on top of chaos. The outdoor display struggle is a real-life version of the old radio game, "Can You Top This?" The process demands the heaping of one excess upon the other in order merely to stand still in the race for attention.

The term "sign control" throws many businessmen into a fit, and this is unfortunate, for the fact is that sign control does not mean economic loss, as the shopkeepers of Menlo Park, Carmel, La Jolla, Santa Barbara and Palm Springs, among other towns, will testify. These towns and a few counties, including Marin, Monterey and Santa Barbara, have already written laws that should stand as inspiration and guide to the eyesore cities and counties most of us are forced to live in.

Effective sign control means more than stamping out the gnatlike Nervous Sign and other grotesqueries of the on-premise advertising world. It means the creation of restrictions on sign size, height, motion, brilliance, etc., all aimed at restoring order to the process of business identification, and eliminating the burdensome, ineffective, strident ugliness we have blindly led ourselves into.

The forces of visual pollution operate, in the absence of controls, under inexorable laws that invariably lead to a chaotic saturation of the roadside wherever the traffic is sufficient to justify the investment. This road is the entrance to San Rafael, which happens to be the seat of Marin County's strongly conservation-oriented government.

Right: Perhaps it is unfair to pick on a town as forlorn as Lancaster for an example of urban billboard pollution, but there it is. Lancaster, situated in middle of northern Los Angeles County's desert country—a section with tremendous potential for agricultural and urban development once water is brought in.

These two billboards, above, on San Francisco's Powell Street were among several score owned by several companies that were first declared illegal or non-conforming by the city attorney in 1937. They were ordered down in 1952; this picture was taken in 1964, they were still up and earning in 1967. The industry's code of ethics forbids billboards in residential districts, partly because there are few residential streets with enough traffic to make billboards worthwhile, partly because a large majority of the public is unsympathetic to billboards *anywhere* (so why make waves where there's so little to gain), and finally, to add credence to the industry's argument that since outdoor advertising is a business, it is un-American to even suggest that billboard control in commercial and industrial zones be exercised. This last, of course, is utter nonsense. Opium peddling is a business, but we don't allow it in commercial and industrial sections. Note the advertising on the cable car. Some town, Frisco.

It wasn't always so, that streets were denied of beauty by endless rows of billboards and on-premise advertising. This was Van Nuys fifty odd years ago. Restraint was a matter of good manners, and wise drygoodsmen and innkeepers knew it was good business to blow their horns softly. Notice the "Hotel Menlo" and "The Van Nuys" signs. Below is the eastern entrance to San Francisco, Queen City of the Pacific.

Los Angeles is probably the most billboard-bedecked city in the world. There are literally hundreds of miles of dreary boulevards like that above (I can't remember whether it was Western or Olympic or Pico, but it matters not, for they all look the same). Even Wilshire Boulevard, the brightest street in town, below, is blighted. The Los Angeles city fathers should take a long look at the stretch of Wilshire that runs through Beverly Hills, where billboards are outlawed, for a good idea of the potential beauty that has been needlessly sacrificed to commercialism.

Someone—no one knows who, and I'm not pointing a finger at anyone—cut down a couple of young sycamores on the Arroyo Seco Parkway in Los Angeles way back in 1950. In each case the trees blocked the view of a billboard. In the picture above, a man holds the top section of the tree in position to create the "before" of a before-and-after sequence. Soon thereafter, the Division of Highways decreed that there would be no more landscaping along freeways unless the communities outlawed billboards along the rights of way. Los Angeles was one of the cities to comply. (The sad thing is: How are you going to meaningfully landscape such horrors as the Santa Monica and San Diego freeways?). Strangely, some freeways in cities

that do permit billboards are landscaped by the Division of Highways under the euphemistic name of "protective planting." Why, I can't say. ("Protection" for whom from what?) The James Lick Freeway in the Candlestick Park section and Interstate 80 in Vallejo, for instance, are handsomely planted with trees, shrubs and billboards. As the plants grow, the billboard folks heighten their signs. The time may come when the motorist will have to look straight up to read the hogwash. The Division of Highways owes it to the public to abide by its own rules, and after an adequate warning period, chop down their spuriously named protective plantings. The warning itself might have a salutary effect on laggard city councils.

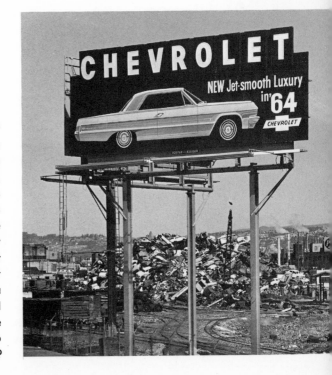

Emeryville, the armpit of Northern California, is site of one of the largest auto graveyards in the world. This pungent scene is viewed by tens of thousands of motorists on the Eastshore Freeway every day. One would think that new-car advertising must surely backfire in a location like this. Or am I wrong in thinking the implications are obvious to all?

This scene is kitty-corner from San Francisco's splendid city hall, and why it is allowed is beyond me. Whisky makers do not or are not allowed to advertise in many magazines or on radio or television. This presumably because of the fear of offending teetotal ladies and impressing the innocent young. One can close up a magazine or switch off the radio or TV if the advertising becomes offensive. One can even boycott the offender if he wants. But children and WCTU members, along with everyone else, have no choice about viewing billboards. In order to avoid them you have to see them first, and even if you turn your head very quickly, they've gotten the message through. And that, after all, is what they're there for. Incidentally, the PG&E billboard, but a tiny part of that monopoly's vast consumer advertising campaign, is paid for directly by gas and electricity users. The Public Utilities Commission allows PG&E to charge advertising as a legitimate expense against operations rather than to require stockholders to pay. The reasoning goes thus: The more electricity sold, the lower the unit rates. The truth is that PG&E's object is not primarily to lower rates, but to increase revenues. There is nothing wrong with increasing revenues by advertising, but the beneficiaries are PG&E shareholders, and they should bear the cost.

In defense against the harshness of our environment, we have conditioned ourselves, I think, to see without emotionally responding to what we see. This is a corner in Los Angeles. Count the pleasant elements of the picture: the gabled roof, the umbrella perhaps, and the hand lettering on the humble little restaurant. The rest is concrete, advertising and electricity. Even the bench is a billboard.

The relationship between billboard companies, billboard-control legislation and politicians is complex and one that has never been given a full airing. The fact is that billboards help elect politicians, and billboard demand exceeds the supply at election time. A law prohibiting billboard advertising by office seekers would be the quickest and easiest way to end the possibility of hanky-panky once and for all. No one would lose in the process.

47

The San Jacinto Mountains in Riverside County rise spectacularly south of Highway 60 near San Gorgonio Pass. It would appear obvious that this scenic asset should have been saved from billboard blight long ago. Under new federal law, these offenders and all the others that line the roadway may come down, but will the county act to incorporate the highway into the scenic highway system? Without county action, larger billboards can and surely will be built 660 feet back from the right-of-way, in full compliance with the very same federal highway beautification legislation.

If there is any kind of outdoor advertising that can be shown to serve the public interest, it is that which gives traveler information. But billboards such as those above and to the right ruin the landscape in the process. There are alternate, orderly ways that food, lodging, recreation, etc., information for the traveler can be dispensed, to the mutual benefit of the purveyor and the consumer, without wrecking the beauty of the countryside.

Below: My heartiest congratulations to the Standard Oil Company, to the agency that placed this ad, and to the billboard company which put it up. They have broken a monopoly. Until this type of promotion came along, the gift of free scenic views came only from God Almighty.

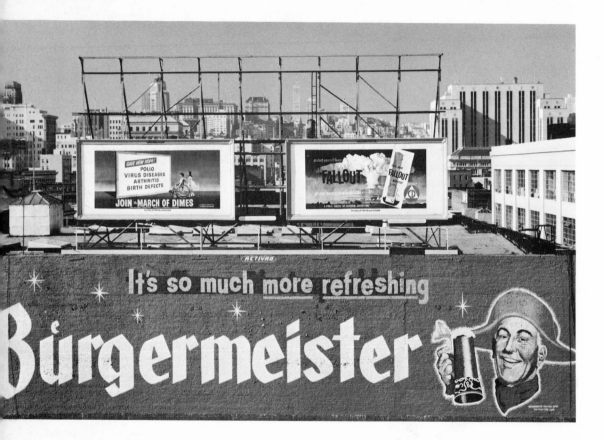

The billboard industry crows a lot about its "public service" advertising—charitable fund raising, safety, "The Family That Prays Together Stays Together" type of do-good promotion, and so on. "We do this voluntarily, without pressure, and this isn't a device calculated to bolster public relations," according to an executive of General Outdoor Advertising. The truth is that the industry donates space because it damned well *has* to in order to maintain that single, narrow pretext of usefulness. The industry also advertises its *own* message in terms such as "Advertising guarantees your right to free choice," in face of the fact that *that* concept is nonsense. Doctors don't advertise, but are we not free to choose among them? Hershey doesn't advertise, but Nestlé's does. Are we freer to buy Nestlé's? PG&E and Pacific Telephone use outdoor advertising extensively, but what choice, pray, is available as alternatives to their offerings?

Oakland's Broadway, above, along with all other commercial boulevards in the old Athens of the West, is lined with rooftop billboards. It has happened almost overnight. Note how billboards enhance San Francisco's Union Square, right. The square, which sits in the center of the city's finest retail and hotel district, is literally ringed with signs, most of them institutional such as these. Their defenders claim that San Francisco would look like East Berlin without them. Below, one of the western approaches to the San Francisco—Oakland Bay Bridge. Again, the brightness of the signs and their cheery messages are described by the industry as elements that give San Francisco its vivacity and allure.

There are some things about Los Angeles for us Northern Californians, even those of us who grittily bend over backwards to be fair, friendly and open-minded, that are very difficult to absorb with equanimity. The voluminous outdoor advertising by Forest Lawn cemetery is one of them. Forest Lawn, the necrophile's Disneyland, is another. I am waiting for the day when the non-surgical pile cure people discover the joys and benefits of outdoor advertising.

There is a fine line to be drawn between billboards and on-premise advertising, at least as far as appearance is concerned, as the view (on the opposite page) of one of California's most celebrated intersections, Hollywood and Vine, may suggest.

On-premise advertising consists of many schools, not the least distinctive of which is a kind of consistently chaotic genre the gas stations have developed. The game is to find the word "gasoline." (It's there, in each case.) Gasoline is a product that sells in the volume it does, not because it is advertised, but because people want to get somewhere and they can't get there without the stuff. Since for all practical purposes all brands of a given octane are the same, each advertises as fiercely as it can for its *share* of the business. The Hancock station, above, across from the State Department of Health headquarters in Berkeley. At the right, the eastern entry to Indio. Below, what appears to be a lottery in northern Santa Clara County.

Three California towns: Santa Monica in the 1870s, above, Colma and Danville in the 1960s, left and below. Compare the efficiency of the signs in terms of *business identification* only between the old style and the new. In the chaos of modern sign competition, the object of on-premise advertising—to describe the business and attract trade—is defeated by the very instruments designed to do the job.

Another example: San Diego's Plaza today, above and in the 1890s, right. The upper picture, a view to the west, was taken from the corner where the old three-story building stood beyond the crowd.

We have come a long way, as the saying goes, but one cannot help but feel, upon viewing such hopelessly self-defeating market-places as Oakland's East Fourteenth Street, below, that we completely lost our sense of direction somewhere in the process. We survive by anesthetizing ourselves, by reflexively ignoring the visual cacophony, and in so doing drive the admen to pile one excess upon another.

San Francisco's resplendent Lombard Street, part of U. S. Highway 101, blares forth

San Pablo Avenue in El Cerrito, left, and Highway 29, St. Helena, above. San Pablo Avenue, which begins in Oakland and courses through Emeryville, Berkeley, Albany, El Cerrito, Richmond, and dwindles out in the sticks of northern Contra Costa County is conceivably the ugliest major thoroughfare in California, Orange County's Garden Grove Boulevard notwithstanding. Highway 29, on the other hand, is one of the loveliest drives in the country, and St. Helena has within its reach the opportunity to become a national showplace. The business district consists of the finest examples of nineteenth century business architecture to be found in the state. Only the twentieth century signs and the mentality that boost and perpetuate them stand in the way.

one more proof of The City's claim to cultural superiority over Los Angeles.

Left, two scenes in San Jose, one of California's oldest cities. It seems to me that the irreverence we show toward our religious symbols is further evidence, sadly, of the role of lip service in religious life. I wonder if you can get to heaven on a credit card.

Right, a section of the grandest boulevard in America's most beautiful city: Market Street in San Francisco. All we need to complete this as a scene from the *Inferno* is to ask PG&E to replace the splendid old light standards with the cold and blinding mercury-vapor units that have already dehumanized hundreds of miles of our city streets.

San Diego, below, or Dago if you want to use the naval diminutive. It's easy to snicker at the déclassé, but what the hell, it's just a matter of money. I find it no more offensive visually than its slicker counterparts.

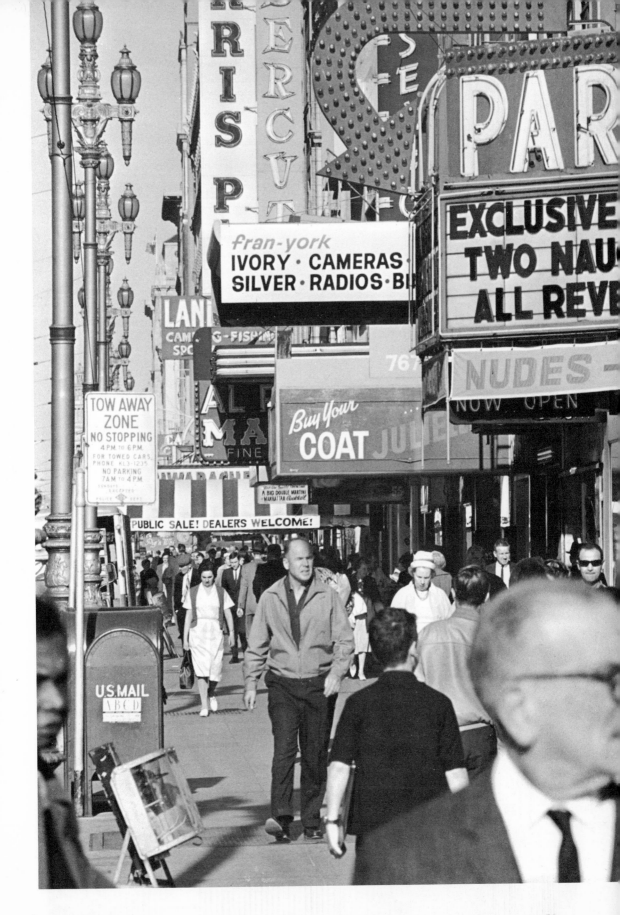

El Camino Real, north of San Diego. Some outdoor advertising gets the message across with penetrating effectiveness—at little cost and without elaboration.

Vine Street, Hollywood. Try as I may, I can't find fault with the groceryman who put Tom Mix up on his "WE NEVER CLOSE" sign. The logic is elusive, but here, somehow, it figures.

One way to get around a billboard ordinance is to put it on wheels and call it a big trailer. This is the intersection of Ashby and Claremont in Berkeley.

Because this neon sign in Belmont is on a place of business, it technically qualifies as on-premise advertising. Functionally, however, it is a billboard and an inexcusable intrusion on the people who live along this street.

Aquatic Park, home of the San Francisco Maritime Museum and Ghirardelli Square, is also home to West Coast Advertising, which has painted its name in type big enough to be read from Alcatraz Island on a foggy day. Another case of functional billboard in a section where billboards are strictly outlawed.

And thus it ever was, that yesterday's glories become today's eyesores. This stuccoed brontosaurus, an oil company's brain child thirty or forty years ago, still stands on the coast in San Luis Obispo County.

This striking car wash is an example of the ultimate in self-advertising architecture. It works so well that no signs at all are needed to attract business. Extreme as it may be, it remains an intriguing, amusing structure.

Two examples of the Disney school of architecture, wherein the building becomes an advertisement for itself. It's atrocious design—phony, dated, child-oriented trash. The fake Polynesian hotel is near Palm Springs and the hamburger stand is in Berkeley.

ALL YOU CAN EAT
$2.39
FEATURING CHOICE PRIME RIBS OF BEEF

Midway

CHUCK WAGON

LUNCHEON DAILY
11:00 TIL 3:30 $1.19 ALL YOU CAN EAT
EXCEPT SUNDAYS & HOLIDAYS

RNITURE CO.

GASLIGHT ROOM PRESENTS
SALMAS BROS.
LIMITED ENGAGEMENT

NO PARKING

San Francisco's Jack Tar Hotel, lovingly dubbed "The Box Disneyland Came In," is not out of place in the carnival atmosphere of Van Ness Avenue. Built with Texas money, the building was originally covered with blue, maroon and cream-colored enameled panels, but driven by repeated cruel jibes in the press, management replaced the maroon panels with blue. Even so, the building still serves as an advertisement for itself. The revolving sign on the roof is an added insult.

The power of on-premise signs to obliterate, physically as well as psychologically, the architecture behind them has contributed to development of architectural poles—shopping-center sterility on one end and Disney-like extremism in which the structure becomes an advertisement for itself, on the other.

Left, a fifty-foot example of the adman's art in San Diego.

Common Trash

All the constituents of litter, from the popsicle bag to the hulk of yesterday's dream car, are the products of our affluence. But more than mere material wealth is required to produce the endless miles of trash and filth that line our streets and highways. The other ingredient: a deep-rooted cultural contempt for the land. There are, to be sure, strong counter-strains in our culture. But today, indifference and contempt are manifestly dominant. And California is surely the showplace of this dominance.

Both of these pictures, on the left and below, were taken in what poet George Sterling called "the cool grey city of love"—San Francisco. Empty lot, left, is in the Western Addition. Below, a typical late afternoon scene at the public library in Civic Center. Worse scenes might be found in Los Angeles, perhaps, but then Los Angeles doesn't claim to be America's most beautiful city.

ONE of the most lamentable truths about California is that almost anyplace where you can walk or drive a car you will find a trail of trash. On the highways and streets, on the beaches, in the high country, in the waters, in the desert and in the parks, we have managed to establish and maintain what must certainly be the most revealing and shameful mess in the civilized world. I have traveled through thirty of the states, Canada, Mexico, and half a dozen European countries, and in none of these places have I seen anything to match the quantity of litter we produce in California.

There must be hundreds of anti-litter ordinances on the books in the Golden State, and if there is any legislation more meaningless and useless, I would like to hear of it.

Littering is, of course, a national problem. The question is why should it be so extreme in California?

One can only speculate, but for one thing, our streets and highways *invite* disrespect.

Our highways are merely "means to ends" —speedways lined with power lines and billboards. As for our city streets, it is almost absurd to tell a person he must not drop a single gum wrapper onto the pavement of a gaudy alley of fluttering pennants, nervous neon, pop architecture and hard-sell billboards. And it would seem that bad habits learned in the cities are carried to the countryside and even on into the wilderness.

Furthermore, we have so much to litter with. There is probably no population that spends as much time eating and drinking on the road. The ubiquitous Foster Freezes, Doggie Diners, Giant Oranges, A & W Root Beer parlors, etc., give out at least six separate pieces of potential litter with each hamburger and milk shake they serve (sandwich bag, napkin, cup, lid, straw and straw cover). So many things are disposable *and* expendable in our affluent society—the candy wrapper, the cigarette pack, the no-deposit bottle, the newspaper, the tin can, and all the rest of the splendid creations of

our packaging industry, not to speak of such American necessities as disposable diapers, disposable nursing bottles, disposable sun hats, disposable popcorn pans, disposable dinner plates, etc.—that it is little wonder we are inundated.

In short, litter is largely the produce of bad manners and affluence. In many poverty-stricken countries, the most depressing slums are free of litter. Why? Because anything burnable, eatable, reusable, will be snatched up the moment it is dropped. But without cultural contempt for the land, however, sheer affluence will not produce the filth we witness in California. Switzerland, for instance, is affluent, but nevertheless unlittered.

Littering is a sport of spoiled kings. Only a rich society can afford to throw so much away. And California is perhaps farther along than other American states in the development of a consuming, waste psychology. Here, technology and mass culture have made their longest strides. The population is new, rootless, often lacking in respect for traditional values. If a man can feel no connection or affection for the earth, then perhaps we cannot expect him to keep it clean.

Even if all this be so, we don't have to live with filth and trash if we don't want to.

Stanford Avenue in Berkeley, one of the city's major east-west thoroughfares.

Left. Two examples of the futility of posting against littering. If there is a NO LITTER sign anywhere in California without an accumulation of trash in the vicinity, it should be listed in the guidebooks. I have never seen one.

There are at least two things we can set out to do now:

We can educate. As our understanding and appreciation of environmental values grow, we will come to regard this as one of those social values that is worth teaching from early childhood, like brushing teeth and washing hands before meals. It will take time, but it can be done.

And we can clean up. The society rich enough to throw away in regal fashion is rich enough to pay someone to pick up after itself.

The extent of our willingness to pay, or, conversely, our failure to pay, for these programs must be viewed as an index to the valuation we place on the beauty of the earth, and in a sense, the degree to which we respect ourselves.

Los Angeles. An example of the deliberate, and almost always illegal, disposal of garbage along the roadside that hard-core litterers practice throughout the state. Garbage dumping is a reminder of, but not a symptom of, a much larger problem we face. Litter and strewn garbage is a form of pollution that can be cleaned up. But the general garbage disposal problem grows faster than the population grows. We can't burn it anymore, and as time goes on we will run out of convenient canyons and, in the case of San Francisco Bay, tidelands to dump it in. Must we destroy these otherwise beautiful canyons and tidelands before we are willing to pay the little extra that modern garbage reducing systems entail?

Putting up signs to prevent the dumping of rubbish is a public activity that has one thing to commend it: It provides work for people who would be otherwise idle. Nothing is really harmed by putting up these signs, except that they seem to work a reverse effect on garbage dumpers. When a sign is placed at a traditional dumping spot, it attracts attention and attests to the convenience of the location that old-time dumpers had known all along. These pictures, from top to bottom, were taken in: Marin County, Russell City and San Francisco.

If illegal litter were not enough, we are forced to live with all kinds of legal litter—such as the debris scattered by the Lake County wrecker, left. The auto bodies, right, were thrown into a gully below a Sonoma County road in an attempt to stabilize the roadbed. Note the cable that holds the wreckage in place. This is a good, but not isolated, example of government-produced mess.

Trash, like tumbleweed, gathers on this roadside fence in the Riverside County desert lands.

Left. Although Santa Monica has declined somewhat from earlier days of glory, there is no excuse for a town this size to tolerate a shameful mess like the one shown here (1964). This road, a major entrance to the city, leads up from State Highway 1 on the beach.

Even our beautiful Sierra Nevada is not spared. Over the years the Sierra Club has sent many volunteer clean-up expeditions into the high country. An example of their work: In 1960 one party removed *four tons* of tin cans from the Bishop Pass route to the John Muir Trail. The situation is shocking proof of our failure as a society to value beauty or, indeed, the earth itself. As critic William Hogan asked, "Who are these slobs? Where are the mountain manners one thought that Americans might now have acquired?"

Mare's Nest

Coyote Point, San Mateo County, left; Alcatraz Avenue, Berkeley, below; East Fourteenth Street, Oakland, right.

THERE is nothing wrong with wires and power poles as such, and if there were no alternatives to our historic methods of power transmission, this chapter would be superfluous. But the land is draped and defiled by hundreds of thousands of miles of power lines; our city streets are spoiled by the same, ever-increasing blight. One wire, or even one great transmission system, is not necessarily bad in itself. However, when the lines grow so thick and when the view is obstructed and the face of the otherwise untouched earth is obscured to the point we have reached in California then something must be said in protest.

The means-to-ends-at-the-lowest-cost philosophy, which guides so much of our technological and commercial life, is the basic culprit here again. That, and plain numbers. The wire mess is growing at an even faster rate than the population. As the economy grows, the per capita consumption of electricity—in homes and industry—grows with it. And if that factor were not in itself enough cause for alarm, we will at some point begin to consume electricity in an ever-increasing proportion to the other sources of heat and power, for no other reason than that the smog problem will force greater curbs on uncontrolled and partially controlled burning of fossil fuels.

There are several remedies that we could employ if and when we demand it, but it should be clearly understood that the public and not the utility companies will bring about the change. The cost of undergrounding and rerouting is going to be passed on to the user if it is to be done at all, and it is folly to think otherwise. The problem, of course, is to find a way of amortizing the cost over a period long enough to spread the burden. Further generations will benefit as much or more than ours, and they should bear their share of the costs. One expert estimated that it would take an increase of about ten percent in our electricity bill over the next twenty years to underground all existing facilities. Surely this is not too great a price.

Ultimately, I would like to think, we will plan our ground transportation system not only for private and high-speed public conveyances, but for electrical power transmission, and perhaps even our communications and bulk fuel transportation systems in great inter-city corridors. But that is a long way off, and in the meantime, we have our work cut out for us.

What are the alternatives to the mess we suffer with today?

In the case of the high-tension transmission lines that link our power sources to the distribution centers, there are two obvious alternatives. One is to underground where no other alternative will work, and this method should be used universally in urban regions as it now is in "downtown" sections.

Undergrounding is probably too expensive a method for the cross-country transmission lines, but the utilities could route their wires in such a way as to create a minimum of visual pollution for the greatest number. This, of course, implies higher construction cost, perhaps higher maintenance costs, greater power loss, and hence a slightly higher power unit cost, but in my eyes, it would be money well spent.

In our cities, we can underground not only high-tension lines, but all distribution lines. There is evidence that public opinion will eventually force all of our overhead wires underground. In a Gallup Poll in 1965, it was shown that seventy percent of the American adult population favored undergrounding in urban areas, and more persons than not were willing to pay extra for it.

If the private companies had any sense at all on the question of undergrounding, they would grasp the opportunity to increase their expenditures, since they are allowed, if not guaranteed, a profit that in most cases ranges close to seven percent of gross sales. If gross sales were boosted by the process of raising rates to pay for undergrounding and rerouting, this would result in more profits, pure and simple. And profits, after all, are what make Southern California Edison and PG&E tick.

We long ago gave away our rivers, which belong to all of us, to the great power companies, and we have given away too much of our skyline in the process. Carey McWilliams wrote in 1949 in *California, The*

Great Exception, that he believed that the state would have to take over the PG&E. I would think there is less likelihood of this today than there was then, although communities such as Redding, Palo Alto and Sacramento, have had the good sense to set up publicly owned electric systems. The threat of converting to public ownership is perhaps the most powerful weapon in the anti-blight arsenal, but it isn't being exploited and we can't count on it to achieve the goal we seek.

Clearly, the great power companies *and* the publicly owned systems must be made to respond to the growing need for relief from visual pollution. And to achieve this, public clamor must grow until the question becomes a statewide political issue. We have quite a way to go yet.

Bryant Street,
San Francisco

In the name of the Father and the Son and the Holy Ghost, Amen.

It's hitting below the belt a bit, I suppose, to show scenes like these, but then Pacific Gas & Electric didn't bother to ask me, or the pastors of these churches, or any of the many public agencies that represent me in dealing with this monopoly if they could put up these blasphemies. (If, in protest, I could buy either my gas or electricity from someone else I would, but I have no choice.) San Francisco, top left and bottom right; Oakland, bottom left; Hoopa Indian Reservation, above.

It would seem to me that we have reached a point in technological development that somehow we should not have to live with this sort of thing. And yet more of it goes up every day. One would think if it were impossible to put the lines underground it would be another matter, but this technology is well developed. Actually, we could, if we pushed hard enough, get the responsible parties to lay every last mile of wire out of sight. Trestle Glen, appropriately named, in Oakland, above; Los Angeles, center left; entrance to Peninsula Sportsmen's Club, San Mateo County. Opposite page, Coyote Point, San Mateo County.

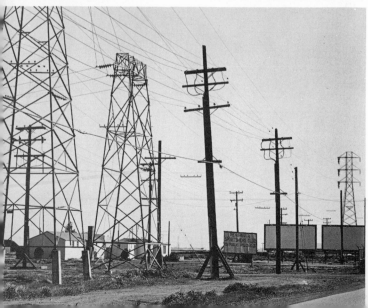

Like our highways, wires
are ends in themselves as
objects in the environment,
yet they are treated as
means alone. We have
allowed the utilities to
strangle our townscapes
all over the state.
Opposite page: Pico
Boulevard, Los Angeles,
above; Los Angeles
Harbor, below; this page,
San Francisco.

Opposite: Berkeley and Los Angeles; San
Francisco above.

Even small towns like Tomales, above, which, being out of the mainstream of progress, have otherwise been untouched by contemporary blight, are draped with blessings of Reddy Kilowatt civilization. But no damage the power companies have done is greater than that to the countryside. The precious San Mateo Hills, below, for example are being violated at an increasing rate, and the protesting public is helpless. Is it our destiny to desecrate every last inch of the face of the land with our works? Is there no way to recover the right we gave the monopolies to defile such priceless public (even though privately owned) values as these serene hills in Contra Costa County? Must these hills someday be festooned with high-tension lines? Perhaps they must (although this is unlikely), but who will make the decision: the engineers of a virtually uncontrolled, privately owned monopoly or the people of California? As matters stand now, the people have no voice in decisions such as these even though the earth belongs to all of us, in spirit if not in fee simple. We gave away control of our skyline when the state was young and land was limit-less, just as we gave away our mountain streams that generate the power. If we are to insure permanent protection of irreplaceable beauty such as this, the Legislature must act now with all speed. It is already very late.

Ticky-Tacky

San Mateo County, below, all of it really lovely country, has been half wrecked by the developers, some of whom are thundering ahead to wreck the other half. Contra Costa County, left, which has undergone perhaps the worst-planned growth in the state has given its shoreline and most of its water-view land over to industry and already half of its rich agricultural land over to housing like that which is pictured here. Study the ingredients of the backyard scene: dog, barbecue, barbecue bench and table, aluminum and plastic chaise lounges, concrete patio, redwood fence. Pure, undiluted California "outdoor living." Row housing, Pacifica, right.

"THE truth of beauty is to be found in a beautiful people, reflecting the happiness and pleasure that comes from living in and identifying themselves with an environment that offers opportunities to enjoy a full and pleasant life, one that makes it possible for each person to point with pride to 'his' community—and to inspire each citizen to have as one of his personal goals the desire, in the terms of the Athenian Oath, to leave his city a better place for having had the privilege of living there."

These are the words of Planner Simon Eisner, taken from his reflective proposal, "Planning Approach to Beauty." He paints a vision of what California might have been, might still become, but not of what it is.

The plain truth is that we have polluted the California landscape in the years since World War II with an aggregation of shoddy construction. Much of our tract housing is best described as *schlock*—flashy, shabby goods. The stuff is merchandised in the manner of color TV and the automobile—with the promise of fulfillment and success and prestige and happiness. Low down, easy payments. We have bought the idea that the good life comes in a package.

The quality of construction of lower-priced housing is so bad that much of it will be ready for urban renewal by the time the mortgages are paid off, or even sooner. I have seen suburban neighborhoods where the houses couldn't have been more than ten or fifteen years old that can only be described as slums—lawns gone to seed, broken windows, peeling paint, cars up on blocks in the driveway, littered and oil-stained pavements—all pride gone, broken dreams.

It takes no gift of prophecy to say that the poor, indeed, are inheriting the worst of what we have built, and they will watch it crumble.

And the *schlock* is not limited to housing. The design and construction quality of our shopping centers, motels, schools and other public buildings and high-rise apartment and office buildings is generally no better. We have built tens of thousands of two- and three-story frame apartment houses with walls and ceilings so thin that unmis-takable sounds, including the most intimate and embarrassing, are unavoidably shared by adjacent neighbors. If privacy is not a basic necessity of civilization, what is?

Our public buildings, as a class, are disgraceful. Most of them are characterless hulks that are designed to look as though they provide the most floor space for the dollar. (Often they don't.) Instead of building structures commensurate with our wealth and ability, instead of works of art, instead of landmarks of great quality, we have built monumental trivia.

We have lost some of our sense of the continuity of generations—of things permanent and things transitory. Our world has become overwhelmingly transitory. When our landmarks get in the way of progress we destroy them. We replace our landmarks, and our farms, and our quiet country roadsides with disposable housing and self-advertising commercial structures—almost all of which lack the beauty and character necessary to evoke the feeling of community pride and identification.

We are the most mobile society in the "civilized" world, so mobile indeed that we buy and sell our homes with no more emotion than we attach to buying and selling cars. And this very mobility further detaches us from the affection for community and tradition that must underlie any civilization.

It was Russell Kirk, I believe, who once said, "Ugly towns breed ugly tempers," and then quoted Edmund Burke to express the converse. "For us to love our country, our country should be lovely." Ugliness, like heat and noise, works a great hardship on man, and the tensions that rise in a hostile environment produce an incalculable loss manifested in mental illness, alcoholism, divorce, malingering, juvenile delinquency and the like. And of all the elements of our environment, none is as important as that thing called "home."

But last year's model homes don't look as good as this year's, and the compulsion to move on to something better, to one more promise of the good life, stirs in the Californian's breast. "What is home?" a little girl was asked. "Home is where you watch TV," she answered.

A long time ago we made the error of allowing the money-lending and real-estate industries, aided by the FHA, local governments, and the advertising industry, to control architectural design and community planning and development. We have developed a structural pop art that still carries the name "architecture." The rules of the lenders precluded experimentation, and demanded conformance with *schlock* standards.

We can't blame the architects for most of what we find, because in fact they don't call the shots. "Of course we design *schlock*," one of my architect friends said when I told him of my observations. "We have to design *schlock*. We have no choice." Just as most engineers are incapable of understanding qualitative community values involved in the road-building process, the merchants of our pop-art construction lack the intellect, training, talent and sympathy which are an absolute necessity if we are to create dwellings and cities that will generate love of community. As long as we depend upon the developers, the real-estate hustlers, the bankers and the savings-and-loan folks to guide our development, we will see more of the same sad monotony and Disney-inspired sham that marks too much of our urban landscape.

There are no easy answers to the questions these observations raise, for the roots of the trouble lie deep within our culture and our economic process. I must believe that our educational system ultimately will produce generations of young people who will demand quality and will be filled with the energy and imagination it will take to transform our communities into the great exhilarating complexes they could become. But wishing won't make it happen.

To begin with, if we are to do anything, we should be exploring ways to tap the great reservoir of architectural talent that we have developed in America. Too much of it lies wasted. We could drastically upgrade construction standards and guarantee fifty- to sixty-year loans at low interest rates to spread the cost of high-quality construction. We could, perhaps, call upon the aero-

There were 362 "homes" built in 1958 and 1959 in the Grand Oaks Unit No. 3 subdivision east of Sacramento. Low down, low monthly payments. Castles in the country. The builders took their money and moved on, and from then on it was all down hill. You can look into the backyards of some of the houses from Interstate 80 and read the brief, unhappy history of the tract. In the years from 1959 to 1965, lenders foreclosed on 125 "homeowners."

space industry to work with our architects in seeking ways to use our ever-growing technology to maximum effectiveness. We can once and for all say to the building trade unions that they will no longer dictate the rules of construction, as alternatives to historic materials and methods are developed. We could abolish the State Division of Architecture and leave the design of public buildings open to competition among private architectural firms. We could demand that ten or twenty percent of the money spent on public buildings be allotted to visual and functional amenities. Every public building could and should be a work of art —prisons included. We must somehow upgrade not only construction standards but design standards. Good design must be made profitable enough to hold its own in the marketplace, and this would imply some sort of public subsidy or incentive system, as a starter.

These are random ideas, means by which we might begin to upgrade the quality of our urban environment. Too much of what we do today is based on the premise that tomorrow will take care of itself. Tomorrow, in fact, will not take care of itself except at great cost to the next generations, and herein lies the ethical question that we must answer. Are we willing to accept the obligation and pay the price it will take to leave our communities and countryside better than we found them?

The Cadillac Plaza Apartments in Pomona, typical of thousands like them all over California.

Above: San Francisco skyline.

This picture (which speaks for itself) was taken in San Leandro, but as anyone who has traveled about California knows, it could have been taken anywhere in the state. One house like this does not describe a tragedy; half a million do.

Many Corte Madera families have a nice view of San Francisco Bay. In the picture above, San Quentin Prison casts a cheery reflection on placid waters. Air conditioners, vital to survival, in a tidy Fresno row development, left. Below: North Bay wine country under development; opposite, a silent tract in Hanford, below. The builder built, but no one bought.

LITTLE BOXES

Words and music by Malvina Reynolds

1. Lit-tle box-es on the hill-side, Lit-tle box-es made of tick-y tack-y, Lit-tle box-es on the hill-side, Lit-tle box-es all the same, There's a green one and a pink one, And a blue one and a yel-low one, And they're all made out of tick-y tack-y, And they all look just the same.

And the people in the houses
All went to the university,
Where they were put in boxes
And they came out all the same,
And there's doctors, and there's lawyers,
And business executives,
And they're all made out of ticky-tacky,
And they all look just the same.

And they all play on the golf course
And drink their martinis dry,
And they all have pretty children
And the children go to school,
And the children go to summer camp
And then to the university
Where they are put in boxes
And they come out all the same.

Little boxes on the hillside,
Little boxes made of ticky-tacky,
Little boxes on the hillside,
Little boxes all the same,
And the boys go into business
And marry and raise a family
In boxes made of ticky-tacky
And they all look just the same.

In no type of building do
the standards that are
supposed to establish
quality fail so abysmally
as in apartment house
construction. This structure
is not the minimum allowed:
the garages and the
staircase are enclosed.
Where is it? Berkeley,
seat of the University, a
town that should know
better. The example below
comes close to being the
minimum construction the law
allows. It's in Berkeley, too.

All over California old neighborhoods yield to the new. And because the old neighborhoods are closer to the central city, the new neighborhood is invariably multiple dwelling. This is Los Angeles. It will be interesting to watch as the years go on whether the lifespan of the new construction will match that of the old.

Looming above the California School of Beauty Culture is San Francisco's new Hilton Hotel, a superb example of privately built steel and concrete ticky-tacky.

Sacramento's new Capital Mall. Where once a row of gorgeous elms grew we have light standards and traffic signals. There is an eerie lifelessness to the street, and the architecture, which varies from attractive to incredibly ugly (note the State Employment Building on the left, a prime example of institutional ticky-tacky), makes not a city street, but a sterile canyon. The mall replaced a run-down strip that perhaps needed replacing, but it is not an improvement on the old. It is merely a change. (I can remember people, obviously poor, sitting in the evening on the front stairs of their old frame houses, watching the endless stream of traffic go by. I wonder where those families are today.)

The West Covina Center is not a bad example of contemporary suburban California shopping center, in fact without the sign it is indistinguishable from the hundreds of others that grace the land. To say that it is not a bad example is not to say that it is not bad. There are exceptions to the rule (Palo Alto's Town and Country Village comes to mind), but as a general proposition, California shopping centers are ugly and mean, a sad reflection of the quality of our civilization.

Big Boondoggle

San Francisco's splendid City Hall has been permanently blighted by our latter-day Juggernaut—the State Division of Highways—but it is only one of hundreds of architecturally and/or historically important structures throughout the state that have been or will be marred, blocked from view, or destroyed by the highway builders.

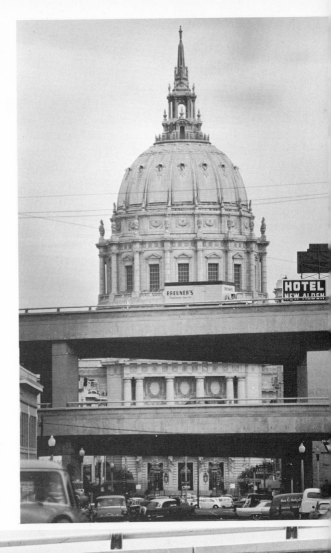

Life magazine, June 20, 1960: "More important than the Dodgers or civic buildings in giving Los Angeles its new personality are ribbons of freeway which are gradually tying the city's scattered pieces together." What a sad commentary. Freeways are popular with most Angelenos, to be sure, but no one can drive through town and view the hundreds and hundreds of miles of concrete, much of it elevated like that shown below, without recognizing the ineradicable ugliness created in the process.

CONSIDERING the mountains of abuse heaped upon the California State Division of Highways in recent years, it seems somehow uncharitable to add to the attack. But add I must, for if past criticism has been severe, it has not gone deep enough nor has it suggested the radical surgery I am convinced is required to create the efficient, pleasant, safe transportation system that we are denied today.

In the last half dozen years, California has emerged as a world-recognized battleground between an outraged citizenry and an omnipotent bureaucracy driven by a single, all-consuming fixation—to build roads that will accommodate more and more motor vehicles at higher and higher speeds to the exclusion of all other modes of transportation. This chapter is full of illustrations of the kinds of destruction the Division of Highways has managed to wreak upon the California landscape.

In sum, parklands have been torn, cities have been shattered and rich agricultural lands have been invaded in the process of building the widely heralded and anxiously awaited 12,500 mile California Freeway System. Of the total, 2177 miles are part of the federal interstate system, ninety percent of which is paid for by Uncle Sam. The balance is financed on a fifty-fifty basis by the state and federal governments. The interstate system, like California's freeway system, is a toll-free network, the reason being that only a little more than one fifth of it will carry enough traffic to pay for itself out of toll revenue. What has been boasted of as "the biggest construction project in history" is without doubt the largest boondoggle in history, too.

It is not the boondoggle aspect, however, that concerns me, but rather those underlying faults in California's highway-building process that have led to the wholesale destruction of resources and values we have witnessed. As I see it, we have made four major errors, all of them understandable but grievous nevertheless.

First, we made the mistake of adopting a "most miles for the dollar" approach to route selection and design. Highway planning is explicitly dominated by the idea

that transportation is merely a means to an end.

Perhaps the most telling indictment against the highway program is the fact that there is not one mile in a hundred that can be considered anything more than a means to an end. You will find no romance, no beauty, no majesty. There will be no sentimental ballad written for Interstate 5. Where in the freeway system can one find that element of nobility characteristic of man's great works of the past? In place of nobility, we find pinched, mean, heavy-handed vulgarity. Instead of a great monument to the genius of American art and technology, we are building a monument to materialism, concrete proof that speed and dollars are the highest values in our culture.

Consider the freeway commuter who for five days a week must travel back and forth, forty-five minutes each way, with the tensions of peak-hour driving, from now until his retirement. His working day—eight hours plus an hour for lunch—and sleeping night—another eight hours—leave him with seven hours to eat his breakfast and dinner, putter around the house, read, watch TV, relax, etc., *and* drive to and from work. The latter item consumes almost a quarter of his free waking time. The road on which he travels could be a thing of beauty, close to the earth and the life that grows upon it. The drive could be a refreshing experience in the morning, a soothing one at the end of the work day. But it will be a cold day in hell before California's Division of Highways and the commercial interests it serves ever produce such a roadway. Not until we change the basic philosophy of "transportation is a means to an end" to "highways and highway travel are ends in themselves" will we see any material shift in highway design. Only when the "most highways for the dollar" concept is replaced by the "best highway for the dollar" will we escape the tyranny of the slide rule and the adding machine.

The second error we made was to build all our freeways, urban and intercity, to accommodate about one half of one percent of the vehicles on the road. The California freeway system, while incidentally accommodating the passenger car and pickup truck, is designed primarily to serve the 17,000-pound-per-axle diesel trucking industry. From the truckers' viewpoint, the "transportation is a means to an end" and "most highways for the dollar" ideas are not only valid, but vital to their interests. Their interests alone.

The truckers claim to pay one third of highway costs, but even if this were so, the public outlay for freeways amounts to a tremendous subsidy of the heavy diesel truck segment of our highway traffic.

No one knows how much extra it costs to build our high-speed roads to big-truck standards, but one high-placed Division of Highways engineer told me, *sotto voce,* that we could build roads for automobiles alone for perhaps one quarter the cost of the high-speed heavy diesel network we are creating. Many special construction factors add to the cost: lane width, depth of the road-bed, strength of elevated structures, radius of curves, size of interchanges, and minimization of grades are among them.

At least the Division of Highways' heavier thinkers appear to have bought the myth that great economic benefits for the general public result from such subsidization, as witness this statement in the Annual Report of the Division of Highways, 1963:

"The time savings offered by freeways are particularly important in commercial operations. Each day, 48,000 tons of goods, the equivalent of 800 sixty-ton railroad cars, are transported over the Hollywood Freeway west of the four-level interchange. Similar tonnages are carried on sections of the San Bernardino, Santa Ana and Harbor Freeways. Lower equipment and labor costs to shippers are reflected in lower prices to consumers."

Stuart L. Hill, a right-of-way agent for State Highway District VII, in Orange County, assured a group of local chamber of commerce leaders not long ago that decreased costs to truckers would be passed on to merchants and thus to customers. "This effect," said Mr. Hill, "is defined as a non-user benefit."

This knee-slapper prompted author Richard Reinhardt to remark:

"If it hadn't been a chamber of commerce gathering, someone might have laughed. I don't know who thought up this definition, which can most charitably be described as a crock of wishful thinking, but it does suggest what one might call user and non-user non-benefits. Among the non-benefits of freeways are the non-taxes that communities non-collect on properties that have been taken for a freeway. Another is the non-existence of forests, beaches, historic monuments that stood in the way. There is the non-productivity of commercial property that is transformed to parking lots to handle the thousands of cars brought into the heart of a city by freeways; and there is also the non-usefulness of a great percentage of urban freeway capacity at non-peak hours."

Although we're stuck with what has been built, and, I presume, with what is on the drawing board today, we are not compelled to continue forever building all our freeways to high-speed truck standards. The Federal Bureau of Public Roads has stated explicitly that low-speed and medium-speed thoroughfares, which would have a greatly lessened impact on fragile landscapes and our cities, can be built with federal funds. We can build roads that follow the contours of the earth, we can build fine webs of depressed medium-speed expressways within our cities, we can build parkways between our cities— all within the law. But not until the domination of big-truck interests is somehow broken will we build the objects of beauty and utility our freeways could be.

Our third error was to have put the highway builders largely beyond our reach and control. In an attempt to keep road building out of politics and to meet post-World War II demand for highways, we created a self-perpetuating juggernaut which under present law answers only to itself and what to date remains a rubber-stamp Highway Commission.

The basic power of the Division of Highways stems from the fact that all fuel tax revenues are, by a provision in the state constitution, turned over to the division to spend on roads. The division is not required, as all other state agencies are, to justify the need for its monies before the legislature.

The result is that as we build more and more freeways we also generate traffic to fill them. As highway traffic grows, more and more fuel taxes are collected, which in turn are used to build more freeways. The process is a vicious, self-defeating circle which forecloses at an ever-increasing rate the possibility of our building an effective multi-mode statewide transportation system which we know *must* be built ultimately.

The first step to correct this error is to wrest control of gas tax revenues from the Division of Highways. It will require a revision to the Constitution, but the time is long since past for such a change. The opposition to such a move will be formidable —the auto, oil, road-building, and trucking industries, to name a few of the more obvious, can be counted on to spend much money to block the proposal.

Gas tax money should be used not only for highways, but alternatives to highways —high-speed surface and subsurface transit systems, for instance, to lessen smog-producing and congestion-making traffic on our city streets. And for that matter there is no reason why gas tax money should not be used for scenic rights of way, and for park-land acquisition.

If the Division of Highways could be required to justify its expenditures before the legislature each year, it would more nearly function, I suspect, as an instrument of the public will, rather than as a tyrant deaf to today's uproar of dissatisfaction and resentment.

The fourth and most understandable error we made in years gone back was to have turned over all aspects of freeway route selection and design to the engineering profession. Of course, engineering is an absolutely necessary element in the road-building process. But engineering proficiency, of which the Division of Highways has plenty, is not all that is required. It is not enough to know how to choose the cheapest route between two points or how to cover that roadway with the cheapest structure adequate to hold up against the punishment of 17,000-pound-per-axle diesel trucks.

Freeways do not exist apart from the world. They go through cities and across the countryside, and even the Division of Highways recognizes the fact that values of a sort that do not lend themselves to narrow economic analysis are important. These "community" values, which involve esthetic, recreational, historic, social, land economic and other considerations, have been ignored partly, perhaps, because of policy, but to a much greater extent because the typical civil engineer is equipped neither by talent, training or sympathy to evaluate them.

The Division of Highways Planning Manual (Section 8-334.1) states, "There are many benefits which cannot be measured quantitatively and therefore cannot be reduced to numbers in an economic analysis. These must be measured by engineering judgment."

Having spent too many years (five) doing editorial bread-and-butter work in the engineering and scientific fields, I can't let this one go unanswered. Of all the professional disciplines we might call upon for judgments of a non-quantitative nature, the *last* one, in my book, would be engineering. Although there are brilliant, articulate, creative men in the engineering profession (indeed, among them are some of the wittiest, most artistic, and most reflective men I know), the great majority of them are intellectually handicapped by processes beyond my understanding. Their ability to abstract the physical world into tidy mathematical descriptions is one of undeniable value, as is the ability to direct a military action or build a rocket to the moon. But just as we do not leave war-making policy to the generals, we should not leave road-building policy to the highway engineers.

Lawrence Halprin, in his book, *Freeways,* states that, "When freeways have failed, it has been because their designers have ignored their form-giving potentials and their inherent qualities as works of art . . ."

Engineering projects can, and indeed often have, turned out to be great works of art—the Golden Gate Bridge comes instantly to mind. But right on the heel of that vision comes the image of the Richmond–San Rafael Bridge—perhaps the ugliest creation of its kind in the nation. Asking the Division of Highways to view freeways as "works of art" is roughly comparable to asking the neophytes of St. Patrick's Seminary in Menlo Park to design the Oroville Dam.

Of freeways, Halprin goes on: "They have been thought of only as traffic carriers, but, in fact, they are a new form of urban sculpture for motion. To fulfill this aim, freeways must be designed by people with great sensitivity not only to structure, but also to the environment; to the effect of freeways on the form of the city; and to the choreography of motion."

Who possesses this "great sensitivity?" Boris Pushkarev, the distinguished architect, proposed in an article in *Landscape* a general approach to the over-all design control problem to which I heartily subscribe. "A highway engineer cannot be a regional planner and an architect at once, but regional planners, economists, sculptors, graphic designers, psychologists, biologists and geologists can work together with the engineer in visual coordination teams to integrate the freeway plan with the over-all development plan of the urbanized landscape, and to make the freeway an enduring work of beauty."

I strongly believe that the architectural profession should be given primary responsibility for future freeway programs. As long as the engineers run the show, we are going to have engineering solutions—more of the same deadly land-wrecking that we witness today. What we must have if freeways are to become the great works of engineering art they could be is an interdisciplinary design control system the likes of which has yet to be produced in America. What could be more fitting than for California to pioneer solutions to a problem that has so long begged attention?

Unwilling to see more of the city wrecked by the Juggernaut, San Francisco's Supervisors blocked a plan to tear up part of Golden Gate Park, despite threats that hundreds of millions of federal dollars budgeted for San Francisco freeways would be spent elsewhere. Robert Bastian pictured anti-freeway sentiment with this cartoon in the May 17, 1964 issue of the San Francisco *Chronicle.*

Oakland's MacArthur Freeway, shown above where it crosses what was once a part of Lakeside Park, knocked out our excellent State Home for Blind, took a corner of Mosswood Park and the Mills College campus, and sliced through the city like a war machine. Heavy trucks are banned because of the noise. The roadway is nevertheless constructed to heavy-truck standards and as such is a monumental piece of overbuilding.

Typical examples of the lifeless, heavy-handed product of the engineering standards books. The structure below looks like a giant reptile squatting over its young.

Transportation is, by definition, a means but our engineers have extended this to mean the freeways themselves are means, not ends. Actually, a freeway is an end in itself as a static object, and one we can hardly avoid. A freeway is also an end in itself as a dynamic environment for the man who must travel it. The time a man spends driving is part of his mortal life—minutes, hours, days, that he will never have to spend again. These hours and days, like *all* of our hours and days, are ends not means. That these hours, year after year should be spent in an environment more hostile than it need be is a tragic waste of life itself.

The Urban Freeway, exemplified here by those of San Francisco, is either so detached from the environment as to exist in a different world or it is so obtrusively superimposed that it overwhelmingly dominates the scene. A freeway cannot be built on human scale in cities as long as engineers design for 70-mile-per-hour speeds and 17,000-pound-per-axle trucks. Freeways that cut cities in two, such as the Alamany Freeway in San Francisco, below right, may have social consequences. In some cities, Fresno and Hanford come to mind, freeways separate predominately white sections from predominately non-white or Spanish-speaking neighborhoods.

Anyone who drives on California's freeways regularly has seen scenes like this. That isn't a cold statistic lying on the pavement in the bottom picture, it's a human body. The state legislature could cut highway deaths sharply if it wanted to, but to date it hasn't shown the guts. In 1965, the state senate shouted down a bill that would have given teeth to drunk-driving laws. Neither radar speed traps nor unmarked cars, both constitutional and either one of which would help greatly to cut deaths, have been given to the Highway Patrol. We *talk* a good safety fight in California, but we don't mean it.

San Francisco, the City-That-Knows-How, has been a freeway battlefield ever since this, the Embarcadero Freeway, was completed. The city has led the nation into a scattered skirmish called the Freeway Revolt, and it took this particularly revolting freeway to do it. The structure completely blocks the city from its eastern waterfront, and stands without a single redeeming architectural feature. The engineers admit that they never would have built it if they could have anticipated the storm it was going to raise. State Senator Randolph Collier, Chairman of the Senate Committee on Transportation, who takes pride in titles such as "Father of the California Freeway System" (how would you like *that* for an epitaph?) said in answer to the constant clamor from San Franciscans, "I don't think the Embarcadero Freeway will ever be torn down. You can't destroy public property." Apparently, however, it's perfectly all right to let freeways destroy irreplaceable community values.

The DOH and the city of San Francisco lost a rare opportunity when they mutually ignored the possibility of taking Geary Boulevard, center, for the cross-town freeway route, which the engineers believe necessary. At the time a sizable section of Geary was widened to eight lanes during Western Addition redevelopment, a simple cut and cover tunnel could have been built. It is too late now. Beyond controversy is the fact that 70-mile-per-hour, truck-sized freeways cannot be built in cities without bringing severe losses, both economic and esthetic.

Freeways are built to accommodate current, and sometimes future, traffic needs. But in addition, freeways also generate traffic that otherwise would not exist. To build more freeways into downtown San Francisco, for example, would be to bring all traffic to a complete halt. This sketch, from the Kaiser Aluminum *News* was done to generate interest and support in the Bay Area Rapid Transit District. BART was voted in by the slenderest margin. Its seventy-five miles of high-speed track will cost more than a billion to build plus another billion in interest on the general obligation bonds floated for construction. And thus critics, including myself, believe that rapid-transit systems that for several reasons cannot be financed with revenue bonds should be financed with some of the Department of Highway's gas-tax money. A change of law, and of course the thinking behind it, will be required before any major shift in transportation planning and construction will be possible. But if highway funds had to be pried from the general fund each year, the Highwaymen might listen a bit more earnestly to their critics. Left, downtown Los Angeles, where already two thirds of the city's surface is devoted to accommodating the auto— streets, parking, or freeway.

Downtown Oakland gives the appearance of being basically a parking lot, interrupted here and there by an office building. Oakland has done much culturally in recent years that San Francisco could well emulate, but in the matter of fighting ugly freeways, Oakland comes out at the foot of the class. The MacArthur and soon-to-be-completed Grove/Shafter Freeways are classic city-wreckers, and in sheer brutishness match anything Los Angeles and other unfortunate Southland cities can offer. .

Even in the country the Juggernaut's handiwork shows its infinite capacity for over-building. Danville freeway left, Ukiah-Calpella section of the Redwood Highway, below. Compare the swathes that represent two new rights-of-way with the existing highways, which in each case are in the upper right-hand corner of the photo. In Lake County the Juggernaut selected a route through prime pear orchards $5 million more in the next 20 years than an alternative route that would have avoided the orchards. The Highwaymen ignored the fact that in 20 years $32 million worth of pears would have been produced on the land they have taken.

Another example of the Juggernaut's propensity for overbuilding. Working with almost unlimited funds, the Highwaymen have contrived to put a fortune into billboard-sized signs such as these. They constitute a conspicuous waste of tax money.

Commute-hour traffic on a typical California freeway. All the cars are headed in the same direction. It is, however, entirely feasible, if a bit complicated, to build reverse-flow freeways that allow maximum use of the high-priced roadbeds. If it can be done at the Caldecott tunnels, right, between Alameda and Contra Costa counties, (four lanes west and two lanes east in the a.m.; vice versa in the p.m.) then it can be done anywhere.

"Esthetics" is a word used frequently by the Highwaymen, but it is abundantly clear they don't know what the term refers to. The pedestrian overpass in the picture above (Los Angeles) is an example of pure, pinch-penny engineering. The overpass on the left was built on the Nevada side of Lake Tahoe and is an example of what a little talent and care will add to an otherwise cheap and unattractive truss structure.

In Sacramento, under the eye of the legislature, the Highwaymen have attempted to build "esthetic" freeways, and nowhere have they better revealed their inherent inability to produce a thing of beauty. By tapering the supports and by adding exposed aggregate panels to some of the approach surfaces they hoped to attract, for once, a little favorable attention. Sadly, as long as we build our roads to existing standards, no frill of any kind is going to cover up the monstrous ugliness thereby generated. Another example of their ineptness was their adoption of State Specification 61G75—a garish green vinyl paint to be used for the finish coat on all state bridges (San Francisco Bay excluded). This ludicrous color was selected *specifically* for "esthetic" reasons. There is a great range of "earth" colors that would do a pleasing job (ask any architect), but Juggernaut Green is not one of them.

EQUESTRIAN PATH

Above is a Division of Highways sketch of a small section of what the Highwaymen expect will become in their words "the world's most beautiful freeway"—the fifty-mile Junipero Serra Freeway in San Mateo and Santa Clara counties. Perhaps it will. But among the criteria that will be used in design are a minimum curve radius of 2000 feet and a maximum grade of four degrees. What this means, in effect, is that the same old cut-and-fill, damn-the-land-contour methods will be followed. A total of four equestrian paths are to be provided under the freeway, each consisting of ". . . graded earth to provide better footing for the horses and to preserve the rustic character of the neighborhood." Rustic character? Roads don't have to be at odds with the earth, as this short section of expressway through San Diego's Balboa Park, below, demonstrates. Built to gentler standards than those used today by the Juggernaut, it fits into—without dominating—the landscape.

The picture to the left is of the Redwood Highway before the Juggernaut rammed through. Although some sections of the old road were preserved, they are so close to the freeway that the leisurely traveler can never get out of earshot of the diesel lumber rigs for whom the new Redwood Highway was built. One of the first sections of the freeway was cut through the Humboldt Redwoods State Park. The Juggernaut, always seeking the soft underbelly, wrecked this park before the public knew what had happened. Parks contain few voters, and this may account for the Highwayman's unusual affinity for such lands. Absolute power to take state parklands may one day be taken from them, however.

Observe the care with which the Department of Public Works built this short section of the Redwood Highway, top right, in 1923. Although the roadbed is too narrow today by any reasonable standard, it remains a good example of what careful engineering can accomplish if proper value is given to the natural landscape. The other two examples show contemporary highway construction in the redwood country. These soils— serpentine, graywacke, broken shale—are unstable, and throughout the region such cuts produce an unending series of slides. This is an abuse we should not allow anyone, public or private, to indulge in. It should be said in defense of the Division of Highways that the damage it does is relatively light compared to that done by the lumber butchers. The power of the lumber industry keeps the heat on the Division. Who can forget that Senator Randolph Collier, head of the Senate Transportation Committee, who represents seven northern lumber counties, referred to the Sierra Club as a bunch of "posy pluckers." In a moment of madness, the Division of Highways proposed in 1965 to name a section of new highway in Contra Costa County the "John Muir Freeway," in honor of the great conservationist and founder of the Sierra Club. Naming a freeway for John Muir is about as appropriate as naming a saloon for Carrie Nation.

It is not steel and concrete that create the ugliness of our highways, it is the way they are used. Compare the means-to-end boredom of the Nimitz Freeway in Oakland, above, with a section of Interstate 5 north of San Diego, top right. Note how separate roadways of the latter undulate and blend with the land. Driving this road gives one a sense of connection with the earth. Driving the Nimitz and its counterparts is hellish. Sadly, Interstate 5 is being rebuilt to the new standards. Compare also the massive cut-and-fill character of Interstate 80 in Contra Costa County, center, with the splendid bridge in the Big Sur country pictured below it. In one case we have wrecked the land to save the truckers a few dollars, in the second we have left the land unruffled and created a work of art upon it. Again, compare the overhead structures on the opposite page, each designed for the same function. One is gentle, echoic; the other, oppressive and pure monotony.

The trucking industry boasts that it pays one third of the cost of highway construction in California. At this they are getting a bargain, another example of "socialism for the rich." Even engineers in the Division of Highways will admit that construction costs for freeways could be cut to twenty-five percent of current expenditures if they had only autos to build for. Trucks account for only about twenty percent of vehicle miles traveled, but for more than fifty percent of the weight carried over the roads. Big trucks, not autos, break up our roadbeds. Admittedly, we're going to go on living with trucks, but why must we tolerate such an outrageous subsidy?

Oakland has banned billboards along its freeways, thereby qualifying the Nimitz Freeway, shown in these two pictures, for landscaping under Division of Highways rules. These two shots show how the public benefits. Signs like those to the left are quite legal and their number grows. No landscaping is possible in most downtown locations, and where it is possible it doesn't do any good. In the picture below we have the freeway, eucalpytus planted by the Division, and in front of them the billboards which, because they are not visible *from* the freeway, are also perfectly legal. All in all, another splendid example of urban beautification.

God bless the man who thought of this. He is worth a thousand engineers and a million miles of freeway, for he brought a smile one day to 50,000 otherwise quietly desperate faces. It would have hurt nothing to leave the sign there, but consciously or unconsciously (I suspect the latter), The Authorities knew that the sign mocked them, they knew this lovely touch of humor was in some way a threat to their Prussian procedures, and so they took it down. I won't forget it as long as I live.

Landwrecking

The damming of Hetch Hetchy Valley in Yosemite National Park more than fifty years ago
is a classic example of destruction of an
irreplaceable natural asset for the sake of
a few dollars. The city of San Francisco
wanted cheap water and this was the cheapest site available. John Muir, who for ten years
battled in vain against the Gothic politicians
and engineers bent on sacrificing the valley,
called it the "Tuolumne Yosemite," because
in his eyes it was the "wonderful exact
counterpart of the Merced Yosemite . . ."
(the Yosemite Valley the world knows).

IN addition to being the world's primary battleground for broader environmental-control issues, California continues to be a veritable cornucopia of smaller, sharply etched resource-destroying processes and projects worth noting. Those pictured and commented on herein are not necessarily the most important that might be gathered, but together they give, I believe, further evidence of our positive genius not only for taking the choicest resources for other than their best uses, but squandering them while we're at it. We are a race of overbuilders, and nothing is sacred—neither soil, nor water, nor air, nor beauty, nor history, nor the plants and animals with whom we share the land.

In an article for the San Francisco *Chronicle* (September 9, 1963), Allan Temko wrote of the striking differences between the Swiss and ourselves in the way we regard and treat our resources. He points out that the Swiss ". . . have long realized that anything done in one part of the nation in-

Despite the availability of many other sources of water, Army Engineer studies showed that San Francisco could get the most for its money at Hetch Hetchy. This single criterion was to prevail despite Muir's immortal reply:

"These temple destroyers, devotees of ravaging commercialism, seem to have a perfect contempt for Nature, and instead of lifting their eyes to the God of the Mountains, lift them to the Almighty Dollar.

"Dam Hetch Hetchy! As well dam for watertanks the people's cathedrals and churches, for no holier temple has ever been consecrated by the heart of man."

The loss of Hetch Hetchy broke his heart and he died a year later.

variably affects the whole. They appreciate, though most Americans still do not, that the mountain wilderness area ultimately is related to the downtown street, that the nation is in the end a single thing—a public thing—which is after all the meaning of the word republic."

He ends by indicting our culture in these words: " 'The land was ours before we were the land's,' wrote Robert Frost in one of his most ambitious poems: 'We gave ourselves outright . . . to the land vaguely realizing westward.' Perhaps, in terms of Manifest Destiny, he was right: the Americans resistlessly occupied the breadth of the continent. But the gift of ourselves to the land was in many ways a selfish gift, and the convenant remains unfulfilled."

Hydraulic mining was the
first massive landwrecking
effort undertaken in
California. Malakoff Diggings,
above, whose weathered
remains stand today as
impressive testimony to
American energy. Some of
the cliffs are 600 feet high.
The main damage caused by
hydraulicking, which the
courts outlawed in 1883,
was to waterways and
valleys below. The diked
riverbed at Marysville,
for example, is seventy
feet above the original
bed because of accumulated
"slickens." San Francisco
Bay was badly silted.
Sacramento, left, during one
of its many nineteenth
century floodings
attributable to the
hydraulickers.

The petroleum industry, indispensable as it may be, is and always has been a landwrecking force. Here, a prime gusher is in the process of wrecking an orange grove in Los Angeles before the turn of the century. Sad as the spectacle may be from the land-conservation standpoint, it is undeniable that no form of landwrecking brings greater gladness to the heart of the landowner.

Market hunters at Clear Lake in 1906. When California joined the Union in 1850, the land, forests and wildlife seemed unlimited. All were there to be taken, to be used. Today duck-hunting is largely a rich man's sport. Little is left of the virgin forest. And we have begun to see that even the land itself, especially our rich agricultural land, is very much limited. The destructive impulse that dominates our use of land and other resources is deeply ingrained in our culture. The job of bringing this impulse under control, or bending the energies behind it to more constructive approaches is becoming a major political issue.

What looks like an open-pit mine is part of a new canal that will carry northern California water south to dry lands and future suburbs. Note the scale of earth-moving equipment. We have the means, money and will to dig great rivers and move mountains. Valuable as this project might be, many earth-moving operations are demonstrably destructive, yet unrestrained by public control. Indeed, some of the worst land wreckage is done by public agencies—notably the dam and highway builders.

Mountain cropping is a process by which builders convert what would otherwise be excellent building sites into ordinary flatland. Right, in northern San Mateo County, the builder has flattened the hills to make better use of mass building methods. It is interesting to remember that the 1906 earthquake, which with fire destroyed most of San Francisco, was caused by a massive shift along the San Andreas fault. Until development began in this section a few years ago, you could still see fences offset eight to ten feet by horizontal displacement of the earth that occurred during the quake. Below, the line of the 1906 rupture runs from the middle of the left-hand edge of the picture diagonally upward to a point about an inch below the top of the right-hand border. These houses are undoubtedly well engineered and built to withstand any future earthquake hazard (I can't imagine the builder not wanting nor the county not demanding this, can you?)

More mountain rework, left, just south of San Francisco in San Mateo County. This type of landwrecking provides something new for California's vaunted "outdoor living"—vertical backyards. Another view of northern San Mateo County, right. Light areas in center of picture are new developments, both adjacent to the San Andreas fault break of 1906. Upper section is that shown on page 137. Lakes in the upper left corner were formed by action of the fault over the ages. Slides along the coast, lower right, were the result of ocean and earthquake action in recent geologic time. When asked if there was any chance that houses along the edge might fall into the ocean during a future earthquake, an outstanding earthquake expert who prefers to remain anonymous said, "It isn't a question of if, but when."

Sections of the Long Beach/San Pedro waterfront could be the most God-forsaken, dreary, depressing patches of earth in all of California, thanks largely to the petroleum industry, forever indifferent to the mess it creates. A sightseeing cruise boat, below, appears to do a thriving business despite it all.

The tools of change and destruction seem to grow each year. Awesome, ingenious, efficient, the huge and powerful machines are fascinating to watch in action. Without them, destructive processes would advance more slowly, but nonetheless surely. Like the logger's ax, they are but tools. Blame for the carnage belongs to the spoilers and the society that blindly allows them to operate.

Bodega Head was not and never will be a spectacular natural attraction. It is a gentle little section of the continent's edge, lying there to be looked at and no more, until the Pacific Gas and Electric Company quietly bought up the land and announced that it was going to build an experimental atomic reactor on the site. The State Lands Commission (our give-away real estate office) had given the underwater lands on the western edge of the Bay to the county with the proviso they be developed in ten years. PG&E, which often acts as if it alone knows what is best for the people of northern California, proceeded quite within the law to run roughshod, in league with Sonoma County supervisors, over the objections of conservationists and others who were concerned about the hazard of building a reactor next to the San Andreas fault, offshore.

PG&E happily agreed to build a road on the sidelands and, with the law on its side, proceeded to landlock many old waterside cabin owners, thereby adding to their long list of enthusiastic admirers. (The project gave them a cheap place to dump the 660,000 cubic yards of earth to be excavated at the reactor site.) In all, PG&E invested $4 million of their stockholders' money before final approval was granted. As it turned out the AEC failed to give a clear bill of health to the site on the question of earthquake safety, and PG&E was forced to drop the project.

Following bad news from the AEC, PG&E announced it would lease to the county 200 of its 225 acres on the Head for five years at $1 per year for park purposes. The county intends to leave it "as nearly as possible" in a natural state. Unfortunately, the damage is already done. I will miss what was destroyed, though I find it reassuring to see that even a billion-dollar monopoly can make a public ass of itself. If I were a stockholder, however, I might be more concerned about learning who laid the $4 million egg.

Like Bodega Head, the green foothill lands back of Stanford University on the peninsula south of San Francisco did not constitute a spectacular natural wonder. However, they made up the last remaining green belt running east and west between San Francisco and San Jose, and they were beautiful. But growth-minded Stanford, self-styled "Harvard of the West," couldn't resist the temptation to ruin this unique oasis for the sake of AEC dollars which would build and support a two-mile-long linear accelerator. It could have been built anywhere, but despite massive local objection, the landwrecking is done. Above, view toward the west of the once-bright countryside with accelerator site on left. Left, vertical view of a small section during site preparation. Accelerator is visible from several miles of roadway, unmistakable under its shiny aluminum roof.

Private and non-profit private organizations are not the only agencies insensitive to the value of leaving natural beauty untouched. Here for all to see is the permanent scarring of a glorious granite slope, scoured by glaciers in past ice ages, by government road-builders whose only goal is to speed motorists through the country faster. This is the new Tioga Road above Tenaya Lake in Yosemite National Park.

Dying Farmlands

California's coastal flatlands constitute, in aggregate, one of the richest agricultural resources in the world. For every 1000 new Californians, 142 acres of this land is converted to urban use and is thereby taken from food production forever.

145

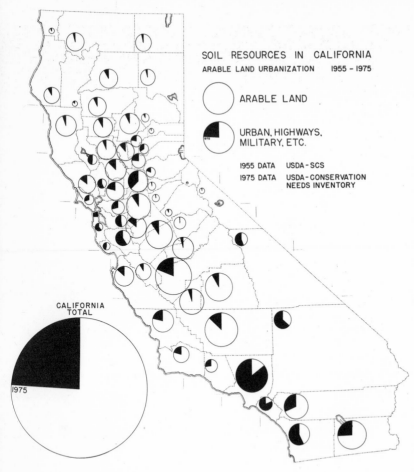

SOIL RESOURCES IN CALIFORNIA
ARABLE LAND URBANIZATION   1955 – 1975

○ ARABLE LAND

● URBAN, HIGHWAYS, MILITARY, ETC.

1955 DATA   USDA - SCS
1975 DATA   USDA - CONSERVATION
             NEEDS INVENTORY

CALIFORNIA
TOTAL

1975

This map shows the percentage of arable land (Classes I through IV on an eight-point scale) that will be urbanized in each of California's fifty-eight counties by 1975 if current growth and urbanization rates remain steady. By that year twenty-five percent of all arable lands will be under concrete and blacktop. The diameter of the circles indicates each county's share of the state's total arable land, and the black sectors indicate the percentage of such lands that will be converted to non-agricultural use.

"ANGLO SAXON, roaring with Protestant scripture and boiled whiskey, changing the face of the earth: felling a tree which took 200 years to grow in order to extract from it a bear or a cupful of wild honey."

These words of William Faulkner's are from *Requiem for a Nun,* published in 1951. While it's unlikely he had California in mind when he wrote, he might well have. Consider the following: The value of California's agricultural product in 1966 was $3.8 billion dollars. (The total value of all gold mined in the state from the time of the Gold Rush to the present is less than $2.5 billion.) On the market shelves and counters the value of this food and fiber was estimated to be in the neighborhood of $12 billion, or about one sixth of California's share of the gross national product. One might think that we would jealously guard this obviously great resource.

But no. Not content with this incredible bounty, we are in the process of literally destroying the lands that make it all possible, and actively boosting this destructive march in the name of progress. With the possible exception of smog and other pollution problems that may prove to have disastrous health effects, California faces no environmental crisis more serious than the uncontrolled, ever-accelerating conversion of prime agricultural land to urban uses.

Agriculture, like fishing, is a process that can be carried on into the reaches of time, provided we husband the land resource. But land "development" is not. We have pioneered in the newest extractive industry— Home Building. The developer tills the land only once and plants houses and concrete. When they are built, he sells them and then moves on to another field and plants more. It is a continuous process that will, in the

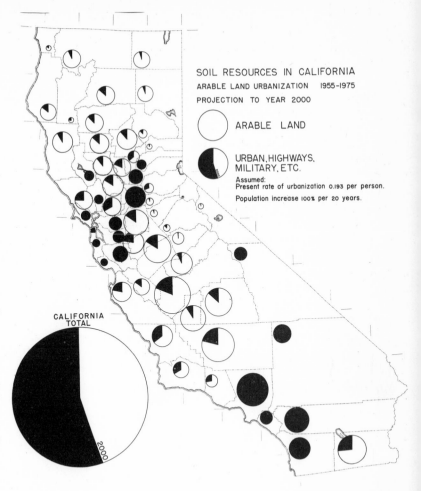

SOIL RESOURCES IN CALIFORNIA
ARABLE LAND URBANIZATION 1955-1975
PROJECTION TO YEAR 2000

○ ARABLE LAND

◑ URBAN, HIGHWAYS,
MILITARY, ETC.

Assumed:
Present rate of urbanization 0.193 per person.
Population increase 100% per 20 years.

CALIFORNIA
TOTAL

2000

Based on the same growth and urbanization rates, this map shows percentage of arable lands that will have been urbanized by the year 2000. Of California's hundred-million-plus acres, 16.5% is arable, including that which has already been converted to non-agricultural use. Barring diminution of growth rate or change in land use patterns, fifty-five percent of those arable lands will have been taken from production at the turn of the century. Again, assuming constant growth and urbanization rates, *all* of California's arable land will be gone before 2020.

absence of controls, continue to devour our rich lands until they are all gone.

If conversion of arable lands continues at the rate we have witnessed in the last twenty years, my children will live to see *all* the state's remaining sixteen million acres of tillable land under asphalt, lawn and concrete. Gone will be the green open spaces. Gone will be the vegetables and fruits and berries and nuts. Gone too will be the last shreds of amenity that made the California countryside the subject of poet and painter for more than 100 years.

It's happening because of apathy, ignorance and stupidity, compounded by fast-buck economics and a population explosion unmatched this side of Asia.

The mystique of Growth has gripped Californians ever since the first pioneers decided to stay and build a new state. Once the railroad was completed, Eastern reaches of the nation were bombarded with California propaganda, in books, magazines, tracts, advertisements, and so on. The railroads and the land developers and the chambers of commerce banged the drum with an unrelenting rhythm and the idea of growth for its own sake, for the sake of presumed profit, growth to fill the boundlessly rich lands of California became accepted as an element of virtue. "Grow or die!" was the cry.

California's population has doubled roughly every twenty years since 1850, the year the state was admitted to the Union. (Every day the total increases by 1500, and 375 acres, mostly farmland, go under.) At this rate, there will be thirty million Californians by 1980, sixty million by 2000 and one hundred twenty million by 2020. These projections, staggering as they are, could be realized, although most experts predict a slowing of the growth rate. (It should be noted, however, that population forecasts for California have proved to be consistently under the mark. In 1950, when the population of California was about 10.6 million, demographers dared to predict an increase of 3.4 million in the following decade. The actual increase was 5.1 million—half again as much.)

When California overtook New York as the nation's largest state a few years ago, no one called the alarm. Most of us noted the event with little emotion, but looking back, I can see that the announcement should have been made in sepulchral tones, and that we should all have worn the crepe.

Already much of our most precious lands, the coastal flatlands, are gone or going. The rich plains of Los Angeles, Santa Clara, Orange, Alameda, Contra Costa, San Mateo and Santa Barbara Counties can be written off as dying cropland regions. And San Diego, Ventura, San Luis Obispo, Monterey, Napa and Sonoma Counties are doomed if present land conversion patterns continue.

H. L. Mencken once warned, "the prophesying business is like writing fugues; it is fatal to everyone save the man of absolute genius," but I will nevertheless venture the following: The passing of our rich coastal valleys from agricultural to purely urban uses will come to be generally viewed within the next five or ten years as the greatest environmental tragedy in the history of California.

Not only are the coastal valleys gone or going, the march of progress in the great Central Valley has already covered hundreds of thousands of acres of the state's richest soils. Sacramento and Fresno have grown with Los Angeleno strides, and another dozen or so of the lesser, older agricultural marketing centers have followed suit on a smaller scale. And the same holds true for San Bernardino and Riverside. Air pollution is already present in all of these sections, and because of climatic conditions, it could become an overwhelming problem if the willy-nilly urbanization process continues unchecked. Even if this be so, the threat of loss of prime soils alone should, in any rational society, be sufficient reason for the public to prevent their destruction.

To ignore the problem or to deny its existence, as an alarming number of planners and agricultural academicians do, is to play the game of the agri-businessmen, whose attitude is abysmally short-sighted and self-centered. (Robert DiGiorgio, an officer in the immense California farming company, the DiGiorgio Corporation, told an audience of security analysts in New York that his company looked ahead to the time when their land would become "too valuable" for agriculture.)

But to pretend that we have no choice in the matter is to play the consummate ass. As psychologist Jerome D. Frank wrote in regard to the new social disease he calls Galloping Technology, "Nothing is any longer inevitable. Since everything can be

Land speculation began in California at the time of the Gold Rush and the right to make an unearned increment became a sacred way of life. Santa Monica land sale, right, in the 1870s.

148

accomplished, everything must be deliberately chosen. It is in human power for the first time to achieve a level of welfare exceeding our wildest imaginings or to commit race suicide, slowly or rapidly. The choice rests with us."

Clearly, it is going to take visionary leadership to get the job done. Yet where that leadership has appeared, the public hasn't listened. Assemblyman John C. Williamson, author of the California Land Conservation Act, which was the state's first step toward farmland conservation, and State Senator Fred Farr, author of the successful 1966 "Open Space" constitutional amendment, were both defeated in the Reagan landslide. Karl Belser, perhaps the nation's outstanding regional planner, finally, in January of 1967, after sixteen years of struggling with local politicians and special interests, quit as director of planning for Santa Clara County, sick and tired of the system that wrecked that once-glorious section of California. When voices like Belser's are lost, the outlook grows bleaker.

The arguments for preservation of California's agriculture are not solely economic. To begin with, aside from all else, how can we ignore the incontrovertible fact that world population is today growing faster than food production, or the fact that a world food crisis predicted for the 1980s is already upon us?

But in addition to the food resource and the dollars, our agricultural lands possess another value. Assuming, hopefully, a world of peace and sufficiency, if not plenty, open spaces of any kind will become increasingly valuable to the public. Not only mountains and beaches and deserts, but orchards, grain fields, vineyards, and rolling grasslands will all have a treasured place in the spectrum of our physical environment not yet recognized in today's short-term economic reckoning.

It is foolish to propose the impossible, I suppose, but when only the impossible will suffice, there is no alternative. If we are going to save the bulk of our remaining rich lands, we must pull rabbits out of the hat.

I submit that we should declare that agriculture will remain into perpetuity a major California industry and institution. This means that we must establish policy that will lead to the protection of perhaps eight to ten million acres of prime lands from the encroachment of the developer and the tax assessor.

As a first step, I would urge the creation of an Agricultural Land Resource Commission by the state legislature, and with it a moratorium on development of prime lands until the commission has had sufficient time to evaluate and present recommendations for necessary legislation. The outstanding work of the Bay Conservation and Development Commission could well serve as a model.

During the moratorium period, building on undeveloped land within existing city limits and on agriculturally unsuitable lands would be stimulated. In Santa Clara County, for example, there is enough open land within existing city limits alone to accommodate all the growth anticipated for the next twenty years.

Obviously, if we are to preserve California agriculture, we must create laws that will eventually direct development onto lands that have little agricultural value or potential. Samuel E. Wood, executive director of California Tomorrow, has long advocated putting our new highways and aqueducts at or above the 1500 foot level so that we might build our cities above the smog on lands that are at best marginal. He paints with a broad brush, but his idea is sound and worthy of serious study.

To expect any of this to happen may be the quintescence of optimism, but I feel we must work with the conviction that the impossible can be achieved. Never was there a clearer case of the absolute necessity to make the policy error, if error it be, in the reversible direction. If we save the farmlands and that policy proves wrong, the public, which will have to invest in the saving process, can always regain its investment and more, quite likely much more. But if we maintain the non-policy course on which we now proceed, there can be no turning back. The land will be ruined.

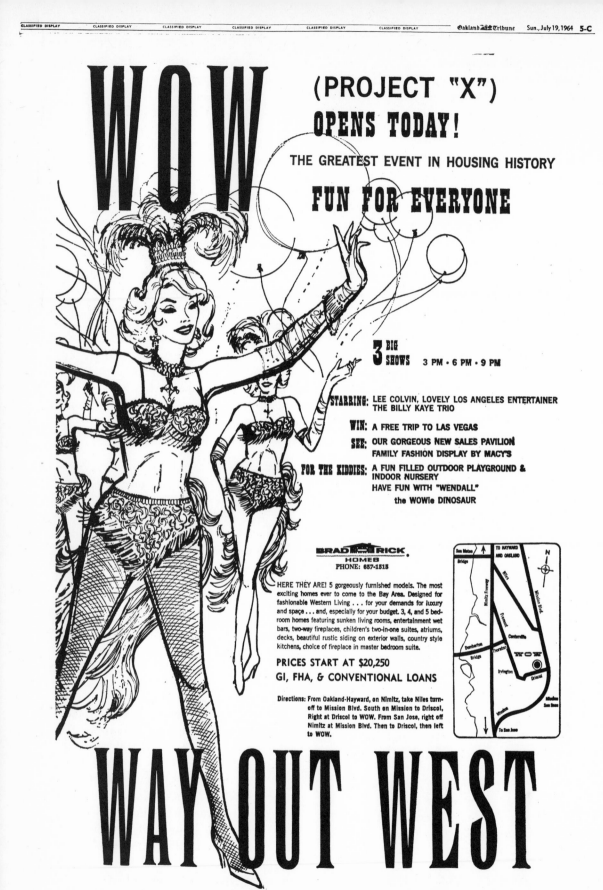

WOW

(PROJECT "X")
OPENS TODAY!

THE GREATEST EVENT IN HOUSING HISTORY

FUN FOR EVERYONE

3 BIG SHOWS   3 PM • 6 PM • 9 PM

STARRING: LEE COLVIN, LOVELY LOS ANGELES ENTERTAINER
THE BILLY KAYE TRIO

WIN: A FREE TRIP TO LAS VEGAS

SEE: OUR GORGEOUS NEW SALES PAVILION
FAMILY FASHION DISPLAY BY MACY'S

FOR THE KIDDIES: A FUN FILLED OUTDOOR PLAYGROUND &
INDOOR NURSERY
HAVE FUN WITH "WENDALL"
the WOWie DINOSAUR

BRAD RICK HOMES
PHONE: 657-1515

HERE THEY ARE! 5 gorgeously furnished models. The most exciting homes ever to come to the Bay Area. Designed for fashionable Western Living . . . for your demands for luxury and space . . . and, especially for your budget. 3, 4, and 5 bedroom homes featuring sunken living rooms, entertainment wet bars, two-way fireplaces, children's two-in-one suites, atriums, decks, beautiful rustic siding on exterior walls, country style kitchens, choice of fireplace in master bedroom suite.

PRICES START AT $20,250
GI, FHA, & CONVENTIONAL LOANS

Directions: From Oakland-Hayward, on Nimitz, take Niles turn-off to Mission Blvd. South on Mission to Driscol, Right at Driscol to WOW. From San Jose, right off Nimitz at Mission Blvd. Then to Driscol, then left to WOW.

WAY OUT WEST

In California, houses are sold like automobiles. This full page ad from the *Oakland Tribune* at first appears to offer something widely appreciated, but, on the commercial market, illicit.

This incredible layout is a "city" near the shores of the Salton Sea—a body of water between the Imperial and Coachella Valleys formed early in the century when the Southern Pacific carelessly let the Colorado River jump its bounds sixty miles away. It is harsh desert land—warm in the winter and punishing in the summer. Property like this is sold by radio and newspaper ads, which offer a free airplane trip and $25 in cash to anyone interested. Note the model homes.

The Santa Clara Valley in my childhood was a vast forest of prune and cherry and apricot trees. When spring came we drove to see the endless sea of blossoms. After the war, developers moved in and did their best to wreck it all. Some day the full story of the greed, corruption, and incredible shortsightedness that accompanied the valley's destruction may be told.

The checkerboarding of the Santa Clara Valley was produced by the raw economics of the process: by leapfrogging over property adjacent to a development one could save money in land costs. The door was open and the horses were stolen before the voice of Karl Belser, Santa Clara County Planning Director from 1952 to 1967 and one of the most forceful and articulate planners in the nation, was heard. Despite the real estate devastation, the county pioneered in the attempt to protect agricultural lands and greenbelting. Left, looking east with San Jose in the distance; right, Los Gatos as it looked when my father was a boy; below, San Jose in smog.

Destruction of agricultural lands reached an ultimate in the Los Angeles basin in the decades following World War II. On this page, Los Angeles in 1874, the year my grandmother, Mabel Knox Bronson, then ten years old, arrived from Oil City, Pennsylvania. Left, the view from San Gabriel toward Los Angeles in the distance. Below, Pico House in the center of town.

Right, Lakewood, an instant community of 70,000 built near Long Beach in the 1950s, and downtown Los Angeles today.

When the first stretch of freeway, above left, was built in Southern Alameda County, almost all of the rich black land was farmed intensely. The little crossroad towns of my memory—Irvington, Alvarado, Mission San Jose, Decoto, Warm Springs, Centerville and others—have been obscured by the housing tide. Still others, like Hayward, San Leandro and newly incorporated Fremont, caught boom fever and have sprawled accordingly. Huge General Motors plant site in preparation just south of the county line, left. Above, the view north to Oakland; San Francisco Bay on the left. All the open lands have been zoned for urban uses.

Contra Costa County's Walnut Creek and Concord areas, part of which is shown left, underwent intense urbanization after the war. All cultivable land and western portions of the county are zoned for urban development. West of Walnut Creek, the Lafayette and Moraga sections, right, have burgeoned. Note how the developers pick land in cultivation for urbanization, while poorer lands lie unused. Below, a view looking north toward Alamo and Danville, two central Contra Costa boom towns, with a disaster called San Ramon Village in the foreground. When the freeway is finished, all of this rich walnut country will be reduced to housing.

Ocean Park and San Luis Obispo County, above; Hollywood and western Marin County, below.

We can keep California green, or at least great tracts of it, if we decide that it is desirable to do so. But it won't happen by itself. There is no question in my mind that new land-use policy must be proposed by the governor and acted upon by the legislature to establish *permanent* agricultural open space throughout the state. Santa Clara Valley, right; the sorry side of Pomona, center; and a lonely farm in the Gabilan Range south of Hollister.

This is California: these are our cities, long ago dimmed by human tears. From top to bottom: San Francisco, Los Angeles, Baldwin Park and Hanford.

This is California: these are typical examples of our open lands, lands that should remain forever open. From top to bottom: Hopland, Central Coast Ranges, Sierra Valley.

A Port Beyond All Praise

San Francisco Bay from the
Berkeley hills.

IF you were asked to dream up the blackest fate possible for the San Francisco Bay Area (aside from the *unthinkable*), could you conceive of anything worse than to allow the powers that be to tear down the mountains and fill the Bay itself? But this is precisely what may happen.

The value of San Francisco Bay—as a port and waterway, as an integral and necessary part of the Bay Area economy, as a recreational treasure house, as the basic element of the region's beauty, and as a vast, untouched open space in the midst of an exploding urban center—cannot be overstated. Who in his right mind would destroy this?

The spoilers are many: small-time politicians, speculators, a few large corporations, the Army Corps of Engineers and the State Division of Highways, to name the worst. Each presumably acts within the law, in good faith, and perhaps with a belief that what they do is for the good of all.

Over the years since the first wave of Anglo-Americans invaded the country, the size of the Bay has been reduced from its original 700 square miles to its present 435 square miles in the process of reclaiming marsh lands for agriculture and diking tide lands for salt production. Almost all of this land is held back by dikes and levees and remains below high-tide level. As of this writing, less than twenty square miles of bay land have actually been filled for urban uses.

But it is not the filling and diking already completed that is my concern (although some of that is certainly to be lamented); it is the filling that will surely come if the state legislature fails to block it.

In October of 1963, the Institute for Governmental Studies at the University of California published Mel Scott's landmark study, *The Future of San Francisco Bay*. This work—a combination of distinguished scholarship and eloquent humanitarian advocacy—is the primary text for all current study and will someday be looked upon as one of the great pieces of conservation literature.

In his study Scott called for a Bay conservation and development commission to be created under a Federal-State-local compact. Without specifying the exact form of the commission, he said:

"It must have authority superior to that of private interests, cities, and counties, and it must be subject only to extraordinary veto by the state and federal governments . . .

"The legal and fiscal powers of the agency must be sufficiently broad to enable it to implement all its policies, but such powers as taxation and eminent domain should be used only in the event the agency cannot obtain the cooperation of other units of government and of private enterprise . . .

"There must be no question of the ability of the bay conservation and development agency to purchase or condemn bay lands. The mistakes of past generations must not be allowed to deny present and future generations their rightful heritage: a superb bay used primarily *as a bay,* for navigation, production of minerals and fisheries, and for recreation and scenic enjoyment."

To the surprise of almost everyone, the legislature acted with remarkable speed and in 1965 created a Bay Conservation and Development Commission. The law put a three-year moratorium on filling and charged the commission to study the Bay and make a report with recommendations for the 1969 session of the legislature. The commission was not given the broad discretionary powers Scott called for, although it does have the right to grant fill permits during the moratorium period. It is essentially a planning body, and under the leadership of Chairman Melvin Lane, Vice-Chairmen Dorothy Erskine and William Evers, Executive Director Joseph Bodovitz, and a distinguished group of commissioners, we can expect an excellent, far-reaching, and I suspect, controversial report.

To better understand the scope and complexity of the questions the commission must deal with, consider the following brief survey published in Spring of 1966 by Save San Francisco Bay Association, the very effective *ad hoc* group that helped push the BCDC legislation through:

Alameda: Dredging and diking for fill continues at Bay Farm Island. A test case raising questions on the legality of the title and the city's proper use of its tidelands has been brought by the Alameda Conservation Association, Box 341, Alameda, which will appreciate any financial contributions for this purpose.

Albany & Emeryville: Filling is continuing in these two cities. However, a strong citizens' group has recently established the Albany Bay Committee which hopes to stop the filling there and improve the proposed waterfront master plan. Both cities claim exemption from control by the BCDC on the ground that projects were started before the effective date. However, there may be decisions by the Attorney General's Office which can legally put these cities under BCDC authority.

Brisbane: What was originally the concern of a small number of citizens is now the concern of the city which has employed Caspar Weinberger to defend its action to prevent the use of Bay at Brisbane as a garbage dump by the Sanitary Fill Corporation.

Corte Madera: Conservation groups in Marin are opposing the creation of a new garbage dump on Corte Madera marshlands. The Board of Supervisors has postponed its decision.

Oakland: The BCDC granted the Bay Area Rapid Transit District permission to dredge the Bay for the proposed tube. Since their contracts to dump the spoils in the Oakland portion of the Bay had been signed with the Port of Oakland before September, the BCDC was unable to take action on the fill, but passed a resolution condemning both the Port and BARTD for filling the Bay to such an extent that the current of water to the South Bay would be seriously diminished. It was announced that federal funds could not be used for any project which would contribute to water pollution. Is BARTD therefore jeopardizing the possibility of securing federal funds? Will the proposed large fill by the Corps of Army Engineers at its Oakland terminal also be curtailed because of this federal policy?

Richmond: The San Pablo Bay Development and Conservation Committee has concluded an extensive study of the shoreline area between Pt. San Pablo and Pt. Pinole, with a recommendation to the city council that a 3-year moratorium be invoked so that further diking for garbage and refuse areas be halted. However, the present dike has never received a permit from the Corps and is thus probably legally within the control of the BCDC.

The City Council recently passed a policy resolution requiring special consideration before a use permit can be issued which will involve a change in land forms, such as quarrying. In addition, Brickyard Cove was designated an area for even more restrictive action regarding grading.

San Bruno Mountain: The owners, Crocker Land Company and the Pacific Air Commerce Center, are completing their plans to substantially lower the mountain—one of the most massive earth moving projects in the world. The dirt is to be sold for marshland and shallow Bay fills such as Leslie Salt Lands and the San Francisco airport.

A grading permit must be secured from the San Mateo County Planning Commission. If appealed by an "aggrieved" party within ten days, it must be brought before the Board of Supervisors.

San Leandro: The city is still engaged in its suit to condemn privately owned property to permit purchase of a larger waterfront recreational area. A new current problem involves the extension of a waterfront garbage dump by the Oakland Scavenger Company.

San Mateo County: Within the next few weeks, 18 city councils within the County will be acting on the proposed revisions of the County Master Plan. Our Association is particularly concerned that the following recommendation of the Bay Front sub-committee be adopted as written:
"A Bay Front Freeway is recognized as undesirable and reference to it should be removed from existing maps but when proven necessary should be constructed with a minimum of land-fill and a maximum of access (through trestles, bridges, tubes, etc.) to properly flush inner water, wildlife and recreational areas; and further, it shall never be proposed as delineating outer limits to any bay filling operations."

And this represents but a small part of the story.

No matter how good the plan is, unfortunately, it will be worthless if the legislature fails to enact programs to back it up. So here we are again, once again, faced with the political realities of our time. We lack the strong regional authority to deal with what is purely a regional problem. The need for regional government to plan and administer those governmental responsibilities that are purely regional is clear. All of our major metropolitan regions desperately need limited regional government to handle at least the most pressing regional problems—air and water pollution, transportation, land use, waste disposal, parks and recreation, among others—and in the case of the San Francisco Bay Area, the Bay itself.

But the question of regional government is one that may take some time to resolve, and the fate of San Francisco Bay can't wait for the answer. The legislature must act swiftly and vigorously as soon as the report is in, for the Bay fill problem is a two-part crisis—the long term and the short term.

The long-term crisis is the specter of an additional 248 square miles of fill, which would leave only 187 square miles of the remaining 435 in open water. If this should happen, and it is legally, technically and economically possible, the Bay would be reduced in effect to a river. But to dwell on this possibility at the expense of meeting head-on, with every weapon we can muster, the short-term crisis would be foolish.

What is the short-term crisis? The most precious of all the Bay lands, the present shoreline, is largely in private hands. Although private ownership constitutes only about twenty-two percent of all the Bay, this ownership embraces virtually all of the shoreline, and with it of course, the most valuable wildlife regions, potential recreational areas, and scenic resources. If we can block this filling of these lands, the long-term crisis will vanish.

There would be no need for outcry if it were not for the fact that the state of California in the past century gave eighty square miles of the Bay to the cities and counties around the Bay and sold another 100 square miles at give-away prices to private interests. If the State of California were to permanently stop the filling of these lands, and there is no legal bar to such action, the threat to the Bay's future and the current raging controversy would end. This is precisely what I propose be done.

If the state has the power to sell and give away in the name of public interest that which belongs to the public, then it has a corollary right and duty to take it back when, because of changing times and conditions it becomes apparent that public interest can best be served by public ownership. For San Francisco Bay the time for public ownership has arrived.

Under the Constitution and the legislation that admitted California to the Union, the state has the right and responsibility to declare that the Bay waters shall remain open. Such a step would precipitate massive legal action, undoubtedly, and perhaps in the end, the state could be required to pay for the Bay lands. Assuming this, what would it cost? Certainly more than the dollar per acre we sold them for. Multiplying the assessed valuation ($5,250,000) of the roughly 100 square miles of Bay lands now privately owned by five ($26,000,000), yields a cost of a little more than $400 per acre. Where in the world could the people of California buy a recreational asset in the center of an urban area of comparable quality? The cry of speculators will be high, but let it be. Speculation in land, solid or underwater, has too long meant sure-fire profits.

What will Santa Fe and Southern Pacific and Standard Oil and Leslie Salt and the others say to such a proposal? It is not likely that they will lie down gracefully, but their interests do not parallel the public's. Leslie Salt's remaining properties need not be purchased outright. For a price, and it shouldn't be much, the state could buy development rights that will forever keep its salt flats in production.

Whatever the arguments, all our urban land needs can be met without further filling, and any argument to the contrary is at best misguided sentiment, but more likely a paid lie.

Suppose we pass up the opportunity to take back that which never should have been taken from the public trust. Who will gain?—a handful of private speculators, a dozen or so large corporations, and a few score petty politicians whose inconsequential domains may be enlarged in the process. Who will lose?—our children. And when all the quick profits are spent and forgotten, our land will lay poorer forever.

The San Francisco Bay Area, were it not
for the waters of the Bay itself, would be
as undistinguished and cheerless as, say, the
San Fernando Valley. No one would willingly
destroy it, but in the absence of controls the
precious tidelands and shallow submerged
lands are being filled bit by bit at an ever-
growing rate. Above, fill project in Alameda
County.

Above, a frozen moment on San Francisco's northern waterfront that tells more about one value of the Bay—call it human or esthetic or spiritual as you will—than all the words in this chapter. Left, tideland garbage dump, one of thirty-odd around the Bay, in Contra Costa County opposite McNear's Point in Marin County.

Because of civic shortsightedness compounded by corruption in the nineteenth century, twenty percent of Bay lands are today in private ownership. If this were not enough, the state has granted an additional twenty-five percent to the cities and counties for "improvement," i.e., filling. Above, fill project at Emeryville, a town so ugly that it has to be seen to be appreciated. Left, dried silt, washed long ago from the logger-ravaged Sierra slope, makes an appropriate bed for the ubiquitous castoff auto tire. Every ugly aspect of San Francisco Bay is directly attributable to man. Those who will profit by filling tidelands disparage the "ugly, garbage-strewn mudflats" as if this were an inherent condition of nature. The Bay, like our forests, is there to be exploited, they seem to say, to be used up, changed forever from its natural state for the sake of private profit or some presumed "public interest."

The aerial view above was taken from Millbrae looking due north to San Francisco. To the west of the straight stretch of freeway is the dumping spot for San Francisco's garbage, Candlestink Cove. In spring of 1965 San Francisco rushed to tie up 135 acres of Southern Pacific-owned tidelands to the east of the freeway to provide a dump for its garbage until the year 1998. But the little town of Brisbane (out of view, left) fought the city in courts, and garbage dumping may be prohibited. But this does not preclude the possibility of filling.

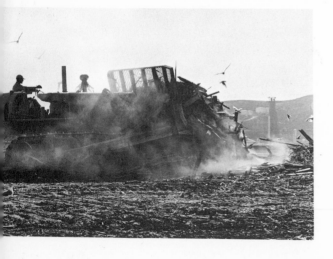

Useful as the bulldozer undeniably is, it remains a tool of destruction. Nothing of beauty was ever fashioned by a bulldozer. Hills and farmlands and forests have all felt its savage bite; now it's the Bay's turn. Whenever you see a bulldozer at work, compare what's being lost with what will be.

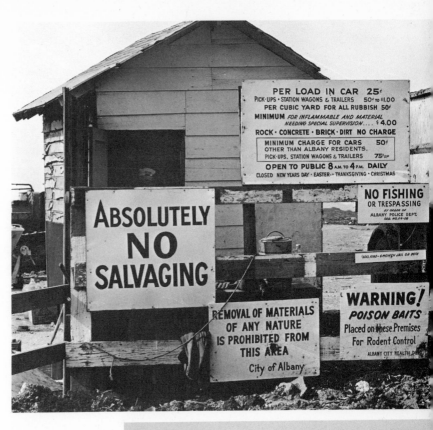

As you can see, Albany is a town with a lot of style. When talk of attempting to control Bay fill first gained public attention in 1963, the city fathers announced that while controls might be desirable elsewhere, Albany was going to fill its tidelands and that was that. The Albany dump and the city's attitude are both the product of Home Rule. The posting of signs like these should remain for always Albany's privilege, but the power to destroy a natural asset—and one that belongs as much to future generations as it does to the present—should not be left in the hands of small-town, growth-loving politicians who can't see beyond the borders of their own town or next year's election. Albany's attitude is but one example of the civic infantilism that pervades too many communities. What San Mateo, right, and Contra Costa counties and the City of Oakland plan, for instance, makes Albany's little project hardly worth worrying about.

In the absence of laws to the contrary, 23 ½ square miles of San Mateo County's salt marshes, tidelands and submerged lands will be converted into dry real estate. The hundred million yards of fill will come from the San Bruno mountains, below, owned by one of the tideland owners, the Crocker Land Company. Other owners include Utah Construction Company, Leslie Salt Company, Southern Pacific, Ideal Cement Company and

several other large corporations. About one quarter of the 23½ miles scheduled for conversion belong to Leslie Salt Company. Much of this is shown above. The county master plan prepared in 1962 proposed that half of these lands be left in a wild state because of their high value to Bay wildlife, and the remainder used for recreation and salt production.

A 146-acre private fill project northwest of Coyote Point, one of the few public beaches on the Bay. This fill cuts off San Mateo County's only unobstructed view of natural shoreline from the freeway and destroys one of the best striped bass trolling sections of the Bay.

San Mateo County's new 3000-acre Foster City, named for the big Oklahoma real estate man developing it, lies on Brewer Island, a reclaimed marshland. In 1964, two U. S. Geological Survey Ph.D. geologists, G. Brent Dalrymple and M. A. Lanphere, testified at Bay fill hearings ". . . the greatest damage in the San Francisco Bay Area at the time of the next major earthquake will be to structures built on made land and marshland adjacent to San Francisco Bay. Furthermore, based on the observed effects of past major earthquakes, we conclude that damage in these areas easily could be of disastrous proportions . . . all development of areas underlain by soft, water-saturated ground, including Bay fill and marshland, [should] be stopped until the problem has been studied in detail and appropriate action in this important matter has been taken by the State of California." Wilsey, Ham and Blair, planners of Foster City described the site thus: "Foster City is underlain by soft compressible organic silty clay to a depth varying from thirty to ninety feet." Foster City's hired soil consultants contested the USGS geologists' statement. Subsequent calls to the USGS by San Mateo's late congressman, Arthur Younger, and his field secretary, George McQueen, who was, interestingly enough, also doing part-time public relations work for Foster City, may not have had anything to do with it, but Dalrymple and Lanphere were subsequently "muzzled" by a directive from headquarters in Washington.

181

Nowhere in the Bay Area is the meeting of
land and water more beautiful than in Marin
County. Nowhere does filling do more harm.
Ten acres of fill in certain sections of the
Marin shore would create a greater loss than
1000 acres in parts of South San Francisco
or San Pablo bays. Marin County supervisors, clearly the best county board in the
Bay region, if not the state, courageously
voted to save Richardson Bay from ruin. But
beautiful waters appear doomed if further
action is not taken. Above right, San Pablo
Bay, which is ringed by five counties, including Marin, and is so shallow that more
than three fourths of it is potentially fillable.
All of the waters of San Rafael Bay, right,
are in private ownership and will, without
laws to prevent it, be filled eventually. Far
right, filled land has narrowed San Rafael
Bay close to town already. Another view of
San Rafael Bay, below, shows the waters that
will someday, without action to the contrary,
be covered with dirt carved from the Marin
hills. Note the dikes and fill to the left. The
destruction will be done in the name of progress. This place of beauty will be destroyed
for the personal and passing profit of a few.

The Bay is many things—a waterway, a fishery, a wildlife refuge, a mineral resource, a tempering influence on Bay Area weather, a sewer, a yachter's paradise, and a garbage dump, among others. It is also one of the most poorly developed playgrounds in the world. Only four miles of the 276 miles of Bay shoreline have been developed as aquatic parks. Fishing, swimming, sunbathing, picnicking, rock-skipping, sand-castle building and plain horsing around are among the diversions the shore was made by nature, or can be made by man, to accommodate. But to the large corporations and syndicates that own most of the precious tidelands and shallows, the Bay is mere real estate only waiting to be filled for housing and industry. And where the cities and counties control the lands, the thinking is, with a few exceptions—Marin and Santa Clara counties, Sausalito, Berkeley, San Leandro, to name the most notable—equally brutish.

The resilience of the human spirit is somehow embodied in our "mud-flat" art. These appealing constructions are made from washed-up or dumped junk that accumulates conspicuously on the Oakland/Emeryville waterfront. This section of the Bay, once the stinking outlet for Oakland's raw sewage, is now threatened to be filled out two and a half miles, 1400 acres in all, by the Corps of Army Engineers and the City of Oakland. If consummated, it would constitute the most horrendous single act of destruction now contemplated for the Bay.

185

San Francisco Bay's swill-eating seagull population grows with the ever-increasing amount of garbage dumped into the Bay, but as the area of the shallow water decreases, the food source for much of the Bay's wildlife decreases with it. If all the shallow parts of the Bay were to be filled, one biologist estimated that anywhere from fifty to seventy-five percent of the birds of the Pacific Flyway would be eliminated. Migrating ducks, right, rest and feed in Bay shallows. San Francisco skyline in the smoggy distance.

Fill projects destroy not only the refuges and feed sources of migratory birds, but those of indigenous shore birds as well. The shallow waters are also breeding grounds for the Bay's fish. In short, if we destroy the shallows we will destroy the Bay's ecology, and as the wildlife diminishes, man's environment becomes harsher. The quality of life is lessened—imperceptibly to many perhaps—but unquestionably.

Mud flats need not be ugly. Indeed in a natural state, unsullied with the castoffs of man, they lie, as shown here at Richardson Bay, in beautiful harmony with the water and the shore. Rich in plant and animal life, the flats are as vital a link in the ecology of the Bay as the shallow off-shore waters. We can afford to sacrifice little of either. Sausalito, right; San Francisco in the distance.

Tahoe Tomorrow

A short stretch of Highway 50 near the Nevada border, part of the five-mile commercial chaos known as the South Shore. Prosperity here depends upon the Nevada gambling industry.

OF all the misfortunes to have befallen California in recent years, none has come with such power to shock and disgust as the wanton desecration of the Tahoe Basin. This dazzling, mile-high Alpine sea is known around the world for its sapphire-blue clarity and for the majesty of its setting. The soaring Sierra peaks; the pines and firs and cedars; the cold, pure waters of the lake itself; the clear air and big sky; the world at peace—all of this and more is the image of Tahoe.

The defilement already produced in the name of progress can be explained, perhaps, but never—not in a thousand generations—will it be justified. And the present desecration is only a hint of what will surely come, barring the enactment of massive curbs on the direction, proportions and style of future development.

The pictures in this chapter indicate something of the quality of development Tahoe has witnessed so far, but to understand the quantity you must extend the view shown on the preceding page along five miles of lakeside highway. The entire length of the south end of the lake has been given over to a seemingly endless repetition of real estate offices, gas stations, motels, frostee-freezes, liquor stores, motor scooter rentals, and all the other drive-in, self-serve emporiums characteristic of our age.

If anyone along this route has attempted, by architectural or landscaping design, to maintain the rustic, Alpine character of the region, his work has been entirely obscured by the mess. Without the backdrop of tree-clad mountains, the South Shore—and to a lesser degree the North Shore—would be indistinguishable from, say, El Camino Real south of San Francisco or Sepulvada Boulevard in San Fernando Valley.

All of what I describe lies on the California side of the state line. On the Nevada side, commercial development is limited, and aside from the garish casinos and a couple of developments, relatively unobtrusive.

It is a sad but plain fact that gambling, which is legal in Nevada, has hastened and shaped the character of development on the California side. A survey taken a few years ago showed that almost forty percent of the tourists arriving by auto at Tahoe were there solely to gamble. The thousands who come each weekend by bus and airline are lured, almost to the man, by the chance to beat the odds.

Gambling itself, however, is not the issue here. I happen to be one of the myriad California suckers who travel to Reno for a fleecing every few years, and I could succumb again to the vision of easy money. But there is a place for everything. Reno is Reno. Las Vegas is to some eyes a great way to make use of an otherwise uninhabitable desert. However, the ideas of a gambling strip to match Vegas on the shores of Lake Tahoe is another matter. It's a blasphemy! Yet it is already well on the way.

The gravest threat facing Tahoe today is pollution—pollution of the lake waters by sewage, raw and treated, and siltation resulting from disruption of the fragile soils of the Basin by developers, and pollution of the land with real estate development.

The battle to come to grips with the sewage problem really began in 1963. It was at this time that outcries against further desecration of the shores and water of the lake echoed through the state. Under the threat of action by the then Secretary of Health, Education and Welfare, California and Nevada began groping for a solution to the problems arising from uncontrolled development in an effort to forestall any action by the federal government. Concern was focused primarily on water pollution. But despite the federal spotlight, nothing of consequence was accomplished for two years.

It wasn't until 1965 that the two states acted to create a Tahoe Joint Study Committee, which was directed to study the problems and to make recommendations for remedial legislation. In Spring of 1967 the committee recommended the creation of a Tahoe Regional Agency with bi-state jurisdiction with responsibility to "preserve and maintain the physical environment of the Lake Tahoe Region, including its natural endowment for recreational and residential purposes, and thus to encourage the economic stability of the region." The committee found the need for legislative action in 1967 "compelling." California passed legislation that will create the agency, if and when Nevada acts, but under the act, control of the agency will remain in the hands of local government. It remains to be seen whether a coalition of local officials—all representing development-minded constituencies—will act in concert to check the interests they have served so well in the past.

Governors Paul Laxalt and Ronald Reagan have repeatedly expressed their concern for control of pollution of the Tahoe Basin, as did Governors Pat Brown and Grant Sawyer before them. But each of the governors talks in generalities suggesting a go-slow, don't-make-waves approach. They deny that the purity of the lake's waters will be irretrievably lost if action is not taken immediately.

The truth is that time *is* running out. Further postponement of action may doom the incredibly blue waters to corruption by dull green and blue-green algae. These simple plants proliferate on nitrate and phosphate ions which remain in all sewage effluent even though the sewage is treated to meet U. S. Public Health Service standards of drinking water quality, and on nutrients washed into the lake from scarred hillsides.

The Tahoe Basin is a natural watershed, and no matter what is done with treated sewage within the Basin—whether it is sprayed on hillsides or run into ditches and wells—it seeps eventually into the lake just as the melting snow and the rain do. The first signs of the process called "eutrophication" have already been found. The algae count is on the rise as a result of increased nitrate and phosphate concentrations. With it comes the inevitable increase in the level of all biological activity. Algae is the food supply of only a small part of the animal life within the lake, but it is a vital part of an unending cycle. As the food supply of one link in the lake's ecology is increased, the food supply of all members of the cycle is thereby eventually increased.

The result is eutrophication, a general biological explosion which once established is self-perpetuating. That is, if we allow Lake Tahoe to turn scummy green, it will never return to the sparkling blue that once inspired poetry and gladdened the heart.

The ideal, simple, economical, common sense, practical way to deal with this problem is plain to everyone. Almost everyone. All sewage in the Basin should be collected, treated to drinking water standards and poured into the Truckee River, which is Lake Tahoe's single outlet. If all of Tahoe's purified sewage were to be dumped into the Truckee, it would today amount to one half of one percent of the river's waters, and only four percent in the year 2010, based on today's population forecasts. But the towns of Reno and Sparks, which tap the Truckee for their water will not hear of it, even though the aerating effect of coursing over fifty miles of rocky river bottom would be more than sufficient if further purification were necessary. The irony of the Reno and Sparks reaction is that they themselves pour partially treated and sometimes raw effluent into the Truckee without concern for users further downstream.

It appears that pumping through or over the mountains to Nevada's Carson Valley for irrigation remains the best quick solution in the face of Reno's and Sparks' stubborn opposition. But for more than ten years the various users of Tahoe and Truckee river waters have struggled to straighten out who gets what. By pumping part of the water (in the form of sewage effluent) from the Basin, the amount left is diminished for the downstream users.

Unless these downstream users will accept less or will arrange to take other water from the area using the effluent, the final settlement on water use may involve a significant lowering of the level of Lake Tahoe in summertime—a possibility that Tahoe property owners have successfully fought for more than fifty years.

It is of course possible that low-cost processes for removal of soluble plant nutrients will be developed. One beguilingly simple process of sewage treatment now in experimental use elsewhere in California converts the organic constituents of sewage into algae, which is harvested, dried, and made into livestock feed. And it is conceivable (although it has never been mentioned, to my knowledge, in connection with the Tahoe problem) that this process could be combined with others as a solution to the complex legal/technical/esthetic water problems of Tahoe. If it could be applied, the clarity and the level of the lake could be maintained without treading on the rights of downstream water users. There would be no need to pump treated sewage out of the Basin.

It's a wild idea, but we are going to need a lot of wild ideas and a lot of departures from tradition if we are to deal effectively with the messy by-products of our technology and burgeoning population.

It remains that Tahoe's water allocation and pollution problems lie well within the reach of technical solution one way or another. But the political solutions are elusive. I seriously doubt that even with regional government the national interest in the Tahoe watershed and the lake itself can be properly safeguarded.

In 1965, Alfred E. Heller wrote in *Cry California:*

"If the purity and beauty of Tahoe are to be saved, we must have an agency powerful enough to knock heads together and get the job done. I would suggest there is such an agency in existence and it is the only one which will be available soon enough to do the job while it can be done. It is the federal government. The President has pledged himself to fight for the natural beauty of America. At Lake Tahoe, as an immediate, interim first step, he could take the pollution situation firmly in hand. In the absence of timely and adequate state programs, he could direct existing federal agencies to adopt a coordinated federal program to prevent the further pollution of Lake Tahoe. I am speaking of such agencies as the Department of Health, Education and Welfare, the Fish and Wildlife Service, the Forest Service, and the Army Corps of Engineers; all have significant authority and responsibility in the Lake Tahoe basin . . . I am convinced that the Department of Health, Education and Welfare alone, today, could close off existing and future sources of pollution, if it had a mind to."

His reasoning and his call for federal action are as valid today as they were in 1965—and the urgency is that much greater.

If it is really in the national interest to preserve the beauty of Lake Tahoe, obviously the job of protecting it cannot be turned over to those who would, because of sheer economic momentum, destroy it.

The politicians who run the five counties surrounding Lake Tahoe are not in office because they are willing to limit or prohibit growth, development, progress and improvement. Their constituents are concerned about getting on in the world.

My intention is not to abuse local politics or politicians as much as it is to expose the underlying weakness of the system. What these counties control at Tahoe today belongs to the nation and to the ages. But neither the nation nor future generations have much of a say in what is being done with that which is, in the broadest sense, theirs.

You cannot, at the same time, build a big city in the Tahoe Basin and preserve its natural beauty. Growth, *per se,* is inimical to our long-term national interest in the Basin, and unless we take the radical stand that further expansion of the gambling industry in the Basin is undesirable, then we might as well forget about "saving" Tahoe.

For as the gambling industry grows, so grows the army of workers and visitors. The Tahoe Basin general plan states that:

"Although the Lake Tahoe area has been a tourist attraction for many decades, intensive use of the Lake Basin by tourists dates from the expansion of gambling casinos at Stateline, Nevada, in the mid-1950s . . .

". . . The most important source of employment in the planning area is the gaming industry. Gambling establishments employed an estimated 2650 persons in July 1960 and 3900 in July 1962. Projected employment in gambling establishments for July 1970 is 10,000 and for July 1980 is 13,500. Gaming will remain the basic industry throughout the planning period."

The likelihood of Nevada's voluntarily

going along with anything that might limit the growth of gambling on its side is remote. And I doubt that real estate developers on either side are yet ready to lie down peacefully in the path of Conservation.

What recourse, then, do we have?

In a footnote to a brilliant article in the *California Law Review* by Carl R. Pagter and Cameron W. Wolfe, Jr., published in August of 1964, called *Lake Tahoe: The Future of a National Asset—Land Use, Water and Pollution,* the authors said:

"An alternative to an expanded interstate compact is the establishment of an autonomous federal agency similar in type to the Tennessee Valley Authority for over-all regional administration of the Lake Tahoe Basin."

If it were politically possible to create such an agency, we might have a chance.

To hope that Congress would create an agency with power to arrest further encroachment is perhaps naïve, but the conclusion is inescapable that such an agency is necessary and desirable. Had the Basin been put aside years back as a national park, a national monument, even a national recreational area, its beauty would have been preserved for all generations.

Before my youngest son is my age, the Tahoe Basin may shelter a million residents and visitors on a normal summer weekend. What will it look like? Will the broad, vaulted sky be clear and the waters blue and the air fresh and pure—a place of singing inspiration, or will it have become a smog trap with slime-filled waters—a gaudy retreat for creatures of the night? One thing is certain, it won't be both.

No corner of California is free of roadside advertising for Nevada casinos. Even billboard interests are a little hard put to define how such advertising serves the public interest.

Not content with the patronage of adults, many of the casinos, such as North Tahoe's Crystal Bay Club, shown here, are wide open to view from the street. It is the rule rather than the exception to see youngsters, perhaps waiting for Mom or Dad, with their faces pressed against the glass to enjoy vicariously the action within. Note reflected scenery. God makes the trees at Tahoe, and man builds monuments to his own greed and folly.

Harvey's, at Stateline, Nevada, was the first of Tahoe's casino-hotels. Among the services Harvey's Club provides is free transportation between the casino and motels on the California side. Two buses stopped for a signal, right. Over the years Nevada gamblers have devised many attractions to draw Californians to the tables—refunds on bus tickets, cut-rate accommodations, free drinks, big-name entertainment, etc.—and have succeeded in convincing many of them that they're getting something for the money they leave behind. It is no exaggeration to say that most Nevadans view Californians with wonder and amusement. The spectacle of a succession of childlike Californians traveling hundreds of miles to lose their money to an unbeatable system is undeniably comic. But the destruction of Tahoe for the sake of this spectacle is a scandalous national tragedy—"Food, Fun, and Fortune" notwithstanding.

195

More South Shore, above. Tahoe faces all the problems associated with rampant urbanization: pollution of the air and the skyline and the water, and destruction of the face of the earth as the ages made it. Until controlled by some agency working to the contrary, the slurb at Tahoe will continue its cancerous advance.

Raw sewage from a malfunctioning South Tahoe treatment plant is dumped into streams that lead back to the lake. In 1967, North Tahoe sewage officials admitted to periodically pouring raw sewage into the lake over a five-year period. Health problems due to sewage disposal are not now critical at Tahoe, but the threat to the clarity of the lake's crystalline blue waters looms larger with every subdivision and high-rise that is approved.

Site of the new Sahara Tahoe skyscraping joy center was once a lustrous, dark-green alpine meadow that sloped ever so gently to the lake's edge.

Had preceding generations had the foresight, the Tahoe basin might have been, as it deserved to be, put aside as a national park. Today, pawn shops are no more out of place at Tahoe than the carnivals, bowling alleys, peewee golf courses and other necessities of the good life that grace the basin.

Land disturbances, wherever they occur—be it for road building, construction or the development of ski areas—are the cause of much of Tahoe's pollution. Left, Ski Incline above Crystal Bay on the Nevada side.

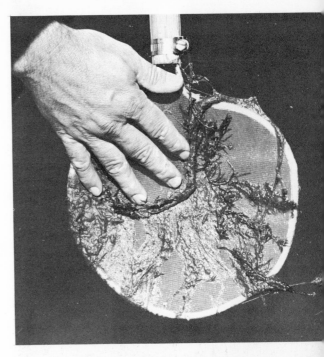

The final, undeniable, omnipresent evidence which gives the lie to those who say the quality of the waters of Lake Tahoe is not being destroyed. These photos were taken in summer of 1967. Tahoe *is* being polluted. Statements to the contrary are, at the very best, wishful thinking and, at their worst, self-serving misrepresentations which work against the vital public interest in one of the world's great natural wonders.

As always, the Division of Highways at Tahoe takes the landwrecking choice if the alternative is either not so straight or more costly. As a result of widening the road above Emerald Bay, as shown here, they have created a scar, clearly visible from the far corner of the lake on the Nevada side, which will take many decades to heal. This is child's play, however, compared with plans the Division has for bridging the mouth of Emerald Bay and for building a four-lane freeway above the present scenic road that carries north-south traffic on the California side. Asking the Division to protect natural values is like giving a butcher a cleaver and asking him to trim your hangnail. The Tahoe Basin highway system should be exempted by whatever means necessary from the destructive standards the Division employs indiscriminately through the state.

Tahoe Keys, built on the sandy flats of the South Shore, is a living example of the insensitivity of those who are in the process of permanently altering Tahoe. This Florida-born approach to land use is, sadly, no more out of place than the overwhelming bulk of all South Shore "development." The outflow of Upper Truckee River shows the effect of land disturbance on the clarity of the waters offshore.

Even Tahoe's North Shore, traditionally more genteel than the southerly end, has collapsed into the same commercial degradation, differing only in extent and intensity. BUSINESS OPPORTUNITIES/TACOS SLUSH TACOS. Is this the end of the American dream? Is this all we are destined to leave for our children?

I have always felt that if I should make it to Paradise I would have to be told I was there. Thus it is at Tahoe. It is bad enough to see our gloriously rich coastal valleys go under, irresistably and senselessly. But Tahoe? Are we determined to accept the ruination of the most beautiful corner of our state for every last fast-buck, landwrecking operation the spoilers can devise?

The Giant Killers

Left, the thick earth-carpet of Prairie Creek Redwoods State Park stands in marked contrast to the tortured landscape of what the Arcata Redwood Company calls a "tree farm."

The desolation shown above right, part of Malarkey Forest near Cresent City, is the work of ravaging loggers driven by a single purpose: to remove every dollar's worth of timber possible without regard to the carnage left behind. This grove had been preserved as a private memorial by former owners. Below, right, the Smith River silently enters Jedediah Smith Redwoods State Park—a 9500-acre remnant of the 2,000,000 acres of redwoods that once covered the Coast Ranges. In 1963 the State Division of Highways, the only agency with power to kill trees in state parks, adopted a freeway route that will leave a mile-long scar across the National Tribute Grove within the park. Although Governor Pat Brown asked the Commission to find routes outside of the redwood state parks, the Reagan administration may view the issue in different light. The threat remains.

ALTHOUGH the first serious proposal for creation of a Redwood National Park was made during World War I, it wasn't until October, 1965, that the first concrete measure was placed before Congress when Representative Jeffery Cohelan of California introduced legislation to authorize the purchase of 77,000 acres of timberlands in Humboldt County, north of Eureka, to be joined with 13,000-acre Prairie Creek Redwoods State Park to form the long-awaited park. On these splendid lands, lying largely in the Redwood Creek watershed, stand the last, best remnants of California's "inexhaustible" redwood forest.

Shortly thereafter, Senator Thomas Kuchel introduced the administration's proposal for a Redwood National Park in Del Norte County east of Crescent City in which 29,000 acres of privately owned lands lying between Jedediah Smith Redwoods and Del Norte Coast Redwoods State Parks were to be combined to create a 42,000-acre park in the Mill Creek watershed.

In the Redwood Creek park plan, 33,000 acres of privately owned virgin redwoods were to be returned to public ownership to be kept for the centuries. Of these 33,000 acres of old growth, 15,400 are owned by Arcata Redwood Company, 16,000 by Georgia-Pacific Corporation, 1330 by Simpson Timber Company and the balance by minor landholders. All of the 7000 acres of privately owned old growth in the Mill Creek park belong to the Miller Redwood Company.

The logging industry, of course, wanted nothing of the sort, but recognizing the overwhelming public sentiment for creation of a Redwood National Park, backed a proposal by Representative Don Clausen of Crescent City which would do scarcely more than link the existing state parks together.

It is unfortunate that the Save-the-Redwoods League, which favored the Mill Creek site, and the Sierra Club, which backed the original National Park Service plans for Redwood Creek, found it impossible to agree on one or the other. Either would have made a splendid park, but the Redwood Creek site was clearly the superior to all but those who argued for expediency.

You see, the original Redwood Creek park plan would possibly have cost as much as two or three times the Mill Creek park. And what with our national effort to create a Napalm National Park across the Pacific, the sympathies of Congress toward such "non-essentials" as another national park tend to wear thin.

Out of this grew the realization that there would be no park without a compromise, and in October, 1967, such a bill was introduced by Senators Thomas Kuchel, Henry Jackson and Alan Bible. Senate Bill 2515 incorporated the best features of the Humboldt and Del Norte park proposals, and it passed the Senate in November by a vote of 77 to 6. The compromise plan, which had the vigorous backing of both the Sierra Club and the Save-the-Redwoods League, embraced 64,000 acres, including, most significantly, about 13,000 acres of superb old-growth redwoods destined for the chain saw.

Be this as it may, the redwood logging industry fought back in response to any respectable park proposal with every weapon, fair and foul, it could lay its hands on. Their spokesmen railed incessantly about the awful damage the parks would wreak on the local economy. They chanted on and on about sustained yield logging and tree farming, and how the parks would destroy the industry. They talked about the rights of private property and invoked the Constitution and even God Almighty.

But beneath all the shouting lay one basic question: Who should get the old giants—the American public, which allowed itself to be cheated out of these incomparable lands before the turn of the century, or the industry which would stand to make many more millions of dollars in the long run if it could keep all the old growth. The industry's front organizations—the California Redwood Association (annual budget 1966, $600,000) and the Redwood Park and Recreation Committee, which was formed solely to fight park plans (annual budget 1966, $50,000)—attempted to block creation of a park of sufficient size and quality to meet National Park Service standards for a single reason: money, plain old money, in the form of dividends and capital accumulation.

My point is not to attack free enterprise or to condemn large profits: it is simply to reveal the lengths to which private interests will go and the methods they are willing to use to protect their particular gold mine, despite the facts and the will of the public. This particular story—the redwood loggers *vs.* the public is a classic of its kind.

The basic argument of the loggers, told with many variations, appeared in an advertisement widely published by the Redwood Park and Recreation Committee:

If these irresponsible redwood park plans were to be adopted, the economy of the northern half of our Congressional District would be irreparably damaged. The growth of the forest products industry would be choked off. Every business in the Redwood Region would suffer. Thousands more acres would come off our Congressional District's tax rolls. Drastic unemployment and higher taxes would be the result.

The fact is that no study supported the industry's contentions with the exception of one: a qualified report by economist H. Dewayne Kreager done on commission for the industry's Redwood Park and Recreation Committee. Every other reliable study showed the park would greatly add to the local economy and that logging at today's rate would end in a handful of years as the last of the old trees go, park or no park.

Gordon Robinson, who spent twenty-seven years with Southern Pacific developing their forest management program and who is now forest consultant to the Sierra Club, projects old growth timber production in Humboldt County for 1970 as follows: 615 million board feet if the park is not established and 565 million board feet with a park. In 1980, his figures are 373 million and 323 million board feet respectively. The effect of a park on second growth operations would be negligible. Richard Q. Siegel, in his 1965 economic study for the Bank of America on the forest products industry in Humboldt, Del Norte and Mendocino Counties, reached the conslusion that employment would be off twenty-five percent in 1975, *without a park*.

It is true that if the Redwood Creek park had been created, Arcata Redwood Company would be put out of the lumber business, but the owners would have been compensated for their property at the fair market price. Georgia-Pacific and Simpson Timber, however, operate a total of 286,000 acres in Humboldt County. Only 46,000 acres of the latter's would have been acquired and of these, only 17,330 acres are virgin stands. Their operations would have continued. The total inventory of conifer forest lands in Humboldt County, preponderately redwood, is well over a million acres. As David Brower, director of the Sierra Club, said, "If the ninety percent of the redwood land they have already logged won't sustain the industry, it won't help them as much as it hurts all of us to let them log the National Park fraction of the last ten percent."

Even the study of local forester John G. Miles, which was published in the anti-park Humboldt *Beacon* on March 10, 1966, confirmed the bleak outlook for lumbering:

In short, maintenance of the present level of cutting for twenty years, principally through liquidation of second-growth, would seriously reduce the sustained yield capacity of the major timber owners. A gradual reduction of the total log usage, from the level of 1280MM (million board feet) per year in 1966 to 900MM per year in 1975, with a further reduction to 750MM per year by 1985, would permit continuous operations at the latter level until 1995 and beyond.

Clearly, the Humboldt County logging industry would be cut back in the next decade or two whether a park were established or not. And once the trees are gone, there is no possibility of a park.

The simple truth is that the North Coast can have its trees and eat them too. A national park, because of increased tourism, will provide an economic base greater than the present logging industry provides and far greater than the projected logging base ten to twenty years hence *with or without* a park.

If Governor Ronald Reagan, who shortly after his election endorsed the ersatz park plan proposed by Congressman Clausen for the loggers, believed the welfare of the people of Humboldt County and the North Coast is identical with the owners of Arcata Redwood Company, Georgia-Pacific and Simpson Timber, he should have considered the following: Georgia-Pacific showed net sales of $575 million in 1965, only a fraction of which was produced in Humboldt County. Georgia-Pacific is a worldwide organization with tens of thousands of shareholders, most of whom never heard of Humboldt County. Simpson Timber Company is tightly held by a Seattle-based firm with extensive holdings in the Northwest. The wages of both companies may be spent locally, but virtually all of the profits leave the county.

But for the fullest understanding of values and interests at stake, the case of Arcata Redwood Company (ARCO) is most instructive. The company was formed solely to cut and mill old-growth redwoods. Unlike the other organizations, ARCO consists of one holding, most of it in old-growth redwood. With the exception of the interest it draws on its large cash reserves, all of its profits are directly accountable to its redwood lumbering activities. And in these profit figures can be found an explanation for the industry's frantic anti-redwood-park campaign.

ARCO was founded in 1939 with a capital investment of $50,000 to which $24,250 was added in 1940. In 1958, ARCO issued 116,690 shares to the Hill-Davis Company, Ltd., a Michigan partnership association which was at the time ARCO's sole stockholder. Thus were ARCO's mill operation and the Hill-Davis timberlands merged. Capital and paid-in surplus were boosted to a total of approximately $3 million. As of March, 1966, the company owned 22,000 acres, of which approximately 4500 were logged over, 15,400 were virgin forest and the balance was in natural meadows and upland grass.

As can be seen in the table at the bottom of this page, the company's financial performance in recent years has been nothing short of spectacular. (All of the figures I quote here, other than my own estimates, have been taken from ARCO's annual reports, and the public records in the Humboldt County tax assessor's office in Eureka and the California State Division of Corporations' offices in San Francisco and Sacramento.)

The sales and net income figures show a trend of tremendous growth—the 1965 earnings were 2.6 times that of three years prior. The ratio of net income to sales has been rising and it's extremely high by any standard. None of the 500 largest industrials in the U.S. show as high a return on sales as ARCO's twenty-nine percent. There are very few over fifteen percent, the highest being eighteen percent, and the median for the paper and wood products industry was six percent in 1965. Over and above the remarkable increase in net assets witnessed in the past, at today's rate the stockholders realize every six years a return (in the form of cash dividends) equal

ARCATA REDWOOD COMPANY
SELECTED FINANCIAL DATA

	1965	1964	1963	1962
Sales	$8,933,342	$8,112,345	$7,390,068	$5,571,885
Net income *after taxes*	2,639,472	2,234,726	1,903,133	1,034,536
Net income as % of sales	29.5%	27.5%	25.8%	18.6%
Net income as % of original invested capital	89%	75%	64%	35%
Net income per share	$22.60	$19.20	$16.30	$8.90
Dividends	$583,450	$495,932	$495,932	$408,415
Dividends per share	$5.00	$4.25	$4.25	$3.50

to their original invested capital of $3 million.

Howard A. Libbey is the only director of the company who lives in Humboldt County. The other directors, as of this writing, live in Washington, Nevada, and Michigan, and Pasadena, San Marino and Atherton, California.

C. Davis Weyerhaeuser of Tacoma is chairman of the board of directors and is reputed to be the largest single stockholder in the company. He is a director of the Weyerhaeuser timber complex. In the monumental history of the Weyerhaeuser family, *Timber and Men* by Ralph Hidy, Frank Hill and Allan Nevins published in 1963, C. Davis Weyerhaeuser is quoted at length only once, and this was on the subject of sustained yield logging, a principle to which ARCO gives great lip service today. In 1935, he . . .

warned that sustained yield must not be thought a panacea for timber management problems. He believed it had "become a fetish, almost worshipped for its own sake," and that it was practicable only when favoring circumstances could be established. *"Too much," he asserted, "cannot be sacrificed today in the way of curtailed income, purely for the sake of assuring a complete continuity of operations."* (emphasis added)

The company has made the claim to support its contention that ARCO has enough old growth timber to sustain its operation until about the year 2010, and that thereafter it will operate on a sustained yield basis. According to Gordon Robinson, the inventory of ARCO's standing timber described on the Humboldt County tax assessor's rolls indicates that if ARCO cuts fifty million board feet per year, the supply will last until about 1986. In 1965, the actual cut was 57.5 million board feet and at that rate, the supply will last until 1984. If ARCO's cut is increased five percent per year (which was the increase between 1964 and 1965), then all the old growth will be down by 1981.

There are several ways the discrepancy between ARCO's claim and the public record might be accounted for. First, ARCO may have plans to reduce its annual "harvest" by half in order to fulfill its own prediction. But since the annual cut has increased in the last several years, this seems unlikely. A second possibility is that the true extent of ARCO's and other lumber companies' timber holdings are not accurately expressed in the tax assessor's books. The third possibility is that the company dreamed up the forty-three-year figure for public relations purposes. But it makes no difference whether ARCO cuts all of its trees in fifteen years or twenty, for the new growth of which ARCO boasts will sustain no logging of any consequence until at least fifty or sixty years have passed.

In 1964, Arcata National Company, a wholly owned subsidiary formed by ARCO, engaged Robert O. Dehlendorf II, who had recently sold a prosperous electronics company which he had developed, to search around the country for investment opportunities. In November, 1965, on his findings, Arcata National purchased outright with ARCO's money the J. W. Clement Company, one of the nation's largest printing firms, for something in excess of $13 million. The company, operating through several subsidiaries, including Pacific Press of Los Angeles and Phillips & Van Orden of San Francisco, prints *Reader's Digest* and most West Coast editions of major national magazines.

It's interesting to note that the Clement Company, whose earnings were *not* included in Arcata's earnings reports, showed a net profit of more than $950,000 for the fiscal year ending June 30, 1965, and approximately $300,000 in the first six months of the 1965–1966 fiscal year. In 1967 the ARCO and Clement operations were combined under the corporate shelter of Arcata National, and we shall never again know exactly how much ARCO's virgin redwood cutting produces in profits.

As the millions pour into ARCO's treasury, it is likely that further "diversification" will be undertaken. In the four-year period between 1962 and 1965, the company sold more timber and timberlands than it purchased. It is odd that such an ardent believer in the sustained yield principle as

It is ironic that most of the land proposed for our Redwoods National Park was once federally owned only to be lost by fraud to a handful of large lumber operators. Steven A. Douglas Puter ("King of the Oregon Land Fraud Gang") is shown above in his jail cell working on his autobiographical book, *Looters of the Public Domain* following his conviction for fraud. Puter began his career in Humboldt County locating valuable stands of redwoods, hiring millhands, itinerants, sailors, schoolteachers—anyone who was willing—to file for homesteads on the lands. As the titles were granted, Puter negotiated sale of the tracts to a ". . . Eureka capitalist for sums ranging from $800 to $1200 per claim. Later, the purchaser sold to the California Redwood Company for $25 per acre. The latter corporation transferred the tract to the Humboldt Mill & Lumber Company, which erected sawmills and commenced the manufacture of the timber into merchantable lumber. At the present time, the timber on these lands possesses an intrinsic value of from $200 to $300 per acre." Millions of acres of our nation's finest forest land were taken in this fashion.

ARCO should not invest its surplus funds in cutover lands which could be reseeded and reforested for future timber supplies. It is particularly odd in light of the fact that profits reinvested in timberlands are not taxed, whereas monies invested in other enterprises are.

The question of how much a park would cost has been tackled by several interested parties—the National Park Service, the Sierra Club, the Save-the-Redwoods League, the redwood industry, and the State of California, among others. The difficulty in negotiations of this sort is finding a basis for establishing a fair market price. In this regard, a most useful figure was established at noon, March 15, 1966, at the Hilton Inn at the San Francisco Airport. The following note appears in the official minutes of the Arcata Redwood Company's board of directors meeting:

RESOLVED, that, on the basis of all facts known to the Board of Directors, including Appraisal of the Arcata Redwood Company Common Stock, dated January 14, 1966, addressed to the Chairman of the Board by Donaldson, Lufkin & Jenrette, Inc., the Board of Directors does hereby determine that on this date the fair market value of the common shares ($10 par value) of the corporation is not more than $360 per share.

If we multiply the 116,690 shares outstanding by this fair market price, which must be considered the company's true evaluation of its assets, the total is approximately $42 million. Of this, the J. W. Clement Company, which would not have to be acquired for park purposes, accounts for $13 million, which would mean Arcata's timber and timberlands, plant and machinery, inventory, and other assets and good will are worth about $29 million. Since more than $4 million of that is working capital, the net outlay for park purchase would be about $25 million.

When Arcata and Hill-Davis merged in 1958, capital and paid-in surplus amounted to something in the neighborhood of $3 million. If the company were purchased today at a price of $30 million, this would mean a ten-time gain on the stock itself, plus the dividends which have been paid out at a generous scale over the years. Furthermore, the stockholders would still own the J. W. Clement Company, which, with its current multimillion dollar plant expansion program, aims at becoming second only to R. R. Donnelley & Sons of Chicago in the contract printing business. Not a bad return by any standard.

But what if the lands are not purchased for the park? Assuming that the company will continue to cut at its 1965 rate and that its profits will remain stable, ARCO will, between 1966 and 1986, realize profits of $52 million. This does not take into account any increase in price for redwood products which may be anticipated as the supply of old growth diminishes. The upturn in redwood prices over the last few years indicates such a trend. When the last tree is down, the company will still own the cutover land which will be worth, at today's prices, at least $100 an acre ($2,-200,000). What they will be worth fifteen to twenty years from now is anyone's guess.

One would think that the directors would have relaxed in the certain knowledge that they and the other stockholders would have made a fortune whether the park was created or not. But this has not been the case. Opposition to the park plans by all the companies remained bitter, misleading, and inflammatory all through the debates.

It is merely a further lesson that business is business, and that we had better not be seduced by the idea that even the best-intentioned men, whose primary job is to produce profits for their stockholders, can be expected to throw away their careers protecting the public interest when it runs contrary to the gathering of the dollar.

Carnage at Berry Glen near Redwood Creek. Arcata Redwood Company's clear cutting destroyed a forest that will take 2000 years to regenerate. Berry Glen lies in the heart of the proposed Redwoods National Park.

The methods have changed over the years, but the object remains the same: extract the age-old wealth and move on. The destruction of America's virgin forests, which began more than 150 years ago, is almost complete.

Logging has always been a wasteful, land-destroying process in America. If scenes such as these taken in the nineteenth century can be excused on the ground that timber resources were believed limitless, similar scenes today cannot. Sadly, the only thing to have changed in intervening years is the power source: the steam donkey gave way to the bulldozer. Despite laws designed to protect our watersheds, erosion has accelerated 100-fold in sections of the redwood country due to abusive logging practices and fire.

Like whalers peeling blubber, ant-like men armed with steel ready 2000-year-old redwood carcasses for the screaming saws of the mill. These irreplaceables went to fill needs that other far less precious timber could have served just as well.

The rate at which big trees are being cut is accelerating as skilled advertising and promotion and the growing population increase the demand for the red heartwood. Every element of the redwood industry economy is growing, except one—the redwood itself. The annual cut is more than a billion board feet greater than the annual growth.

It should surprise most people to learn that we are still cutting the rare giant redwood (Sequoia Gigantea) in the Sierra Nevada. Although this forest cousin of the coast redwood (*Sequoia sempervirens*) produces only low-grade lumber, there is money to be made killing old monarchs like this one. It took thousands of years for this splendid tree to grow. Let alone it might have stood another thousand or two.

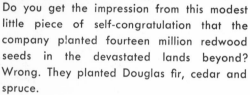

Do you get the impression from this modest little piece of self-congratulation that the company planted fourteen million redwood seeds in the devastated lands beyond? Wrong. They planted Douglas fir, cedar and spruce.

Along the first 150 miles or so of U.S. 101 north of San Francisco there are more signs saying "Redwood Highway" than there are redwood trees. Even the state-owned groves to the north are merely uncut corridors hiding the cutover land beyond from view. Along the roads that lead east and west from 101 lie redwood lands that were wrecked in the early years. Below, grotesque, nether-world growth and erosion celebrate past exploitation.

Fog, which once helped comfort a redwood forest on these slopes east of Eureka, is wasted and meaningless on soils which, without the binding root structures of ancient trees, are slowly slipping into the valley below.

Barren, eroded hills and abandoned sawmills are found throughout the native habitat of the coast redwood. Timber-hungry Mexico and China are fearful examples of man's power to destroy not only forests, but the land itself. Is this to be California's fate?

We hold the power of life and death over everything that grows on earth. How we use this power will determine the quality of life we deed our children. The view above is not a battlefield, it is a tree farm. Compare it with the fallen giant that lies in a bed of tender oxalis, sleeping while the centuries convert its bone and sinew into the raw substances that will help sustain yet another hundred thousand years of growth for *Sequoia sempervirens*—the ever-living redwood.

216

Pass It On

EVER since Sputnik was lifted into orbit, our nation's leaders have stressed the importance of catching up with the Russians in the Space Race. To that end, hundreds of millions of federal dollars have been granted to the public schools to accelerate scientific study. As a result, more children today can accurately draw the concentric circles of the solar system than ever before.

But at the same time, real problems that each child will have to face in regard to the physical environment have remained systematically hidden from him. Just as the public schools don't tell the children of the nineteenth century butchery of California's Indians, neither dare they talk of the twentieth century depredations of the land-wreckers. Indeed, today's spoilers are hailed as champions of progress and of the American Way. Freedom, it would seem, begins with the freedom to destroy irreplaceable assets.

More than fifty years ago John Muir asked a question the people of California have yet to answer: "How long O Lord . . . must the destruction go on?" It has remained unanswered for the simple reason that there have been billions and billions of quick dollars to be made by ignoring it.

For the sake of these dollars we have presided over the destruction of a land blessed with more riches and beauty than most of the rest of the earth. We have methodically cut ourselves away from the land that mothers and nurtures us, and we seem to care not that we are feeding on

CONSERVATION of Resources,

CALIFORNIA

In California

what should have been our children's patrimony.

It seems to me abundantly clear that we have got to stop lying to ourselves and to stop living as if ours were to be the last generation on earth. And one of the giant steps we can take right now is to stop feeding our innocent children the unctuous pap now served them in our public school system.

Let us review the lessons of the chapter, "Saving Our Natural Resources" in *Our California Today*, a standard fourth-grade social science text adopted in 1957:

"Los Angeles has grown into the largest city in California because it is in such a good place. It is the best place in southern California for trade and industry."

"Lumbermen cut forest trees for timber. If they use the forest resources wisely, young trees will grow tall. New trees will be planted. Our forest resources will be renewed."

"Our forests and range lands are now protected. Water is being saved year after year in mountain reservoirs. A farmer can open a canal gate and turn water into his fields. When his son owns the farm, he, too, will have water in his irrigating ditches."

"The lumberman cuts his forest trees for timber. He does his work carefully. While his children are growing up, new trees will be growing up, too. The timber will be renewed. The lumberman's children can make a living from the same forest lands. There will be lumber for new homes in California."

"You have read how Californians save their water, forests, fish, game, and soil. The people of California are saving the renewable resources of our land. When the children of today grow up, they will be able to use and enjoy the resources of our state."

It is obviously high time that we insist that courses in modern conservation be made mandatory in the public schools. If the truth hurts, let it.

The office of State Superintendent of Schools has fallen to Max Rafferty, who, with his degree of Ed.D., has long been a part of the priesthood of the education establishment. In regard to contemporary California, Mr. Rafferty has shown considerable courage by attacking such controversial problems as rioting in the streets, dirty words, unwed motherhood, juvenile delinquency, and student unrest at the University of California at Berkeley. Of education at the latter, he said, "a four year course in drugs, sex and treason."

It wasn't always this way, though. In 1913, Edward Hyatt, then California's State Superintendent of Public Instruction, wrote and gathered material for a small book published for the schools by the State Printing Office called *Conservation of Natural Resources*. To my knowledge, this was the last official work in the field of conservation education with any guts whatsoever. And in the absence of anything even beginning to approach it today, it is well worth quoting from.

Edward Hyatt:

"In no other state or country is such variety and wealth of natural resources to be found as in California. Nowhere else is it being squandered with such careless hand."

"Our boys and girls spend hours and days and weeks in studying intently the virtues and the defects of the Articles of Confederation, dead a hundred years! But they can not discover in their school that men are throwing away and giving away the land and the water upon which the real life of the nation is builded."

"When expressing our indignation at the wicked waste of the people's heritages it is well to remember that it is the people who are to blame for it. You and I and all of us are the criminals, not merely the men and the corporations who have so largely profited by the wasted resources. It is easy to work up wrath and blow off steam about them; but we must remember that they have played the game according to the rules, and that we, the people, make or consent to the rules of the game—the laws. The big boys often try to change the rules and use them unfairly, doubtless, as in smaller games; but if all the other children attend to it, take an interest in it, stick together, they can make the rules right and keep the big fellows within bounds."

"It is well to remember this: most of us, if we could, would do just what the 'predatory rich' have done."

"Our laws are stupid, too, in regard to the dredger industry. They allow capitalists to come into our fertile valleys, pay big prices for fields, orchards, vineyards, and convert them into barren piles of rocks. This makes a temporary prosperity. The owners of the soil get a lot of money, work is plentiful, prices are good—and the capitalist carries away large profits, perhaps. But the brief prosperity passes away in a few years—and what of the land? It is no more! It would have otherwise been producing food, supporting people and paying taxes for four or five hundred years or four or five thousand—but now it is gone. It is a hideous desolation for all time to come."

"There is something wrong in this. It is legal at present, but it is not moral. No one should have a right to destroy the Homes of the future. It is against the general good. We have a right to *use* the land—but not to *destroy* it. It is easily possible to dredge the land in such way that the good soil will remain on top, the cobblestones below—but that costs more money and the profits are cut down. It is also possible that a share of these ill-gotten profits might induce unpatriotic lawyers to hinder and delay the passage of restrictive laws on this matter for many years, while many future homes pass out of the world forever."

"Up to date our stupid laws give away this precious [water] power forever to anyone who wants it, and give him all that he wants, however much—for nothing! Thus we part with our great-grandchildren's birthright and do not even get a mess of pottage in return. The descendants of us who foolishly part with this power now will pay tribute for centuries to the descendants of the men who get it. These Power Lords will rule over the lives and fortunes of the millions of vassals who must have the Power in order to live."

"This Power should be leased, never permanently disposed of. Its title is not rightly vested in us at all. It belongs to the Future. It should never be granted to anyone in perpetuity, but for a term of years, a century, if need be; but in perpetuity, never."

Theodore Roosevelt:

"At our present nice little industrial gait, here in America, we are burning the candle at both ends, quite regardless of the fact that when it is burnt out, it can never be renewed. Such American fortunes as were made out of theft of America's common resources must surely, one day and in some way, pay the price. But let us little fellows who have not "succeeded" in the world see to it that we keep our own hands clean."

"This was a very wonderful and beautiful country. Having seen it before civilization took it all over, perhaps, some of us do not care so much for civilization as we might."

Gifford Pinchot:

"The profoundest duty that lies upon any father is to leave his son with a reasonable equipment for the struggle of life and an untarnished name. So the noblest task that confronts us all today is to leave his country unspotted in honor, and unexhausted in resources, to our descendants, who will be, not less than we, the children of the founders of the republic. I conceive this task to partake of the highest spirit of patriotism."

Benjamin Ide Wheeler, President of the University of California:

"This generation will have for one thing at least a great name in history. Men of the future centuries will surely call it the generation of the great destroyers, and historians and economists will write of the riotous days of nineteen hundred, when the people used up all the petroleum, all the natural gas, all the anthracite and most of the other coal, and most of the handy iron. It will be the period when the forests were cut down or burnt up, the lands stolen, and the waters given away. We are sure to be the subject of earnest remark."

Cardinal Gibbons:

"Our fertile soils, our inland waters, our mines, and our forests are God-given heritages which belong no more to the present generation than to generations that are to come."

Dr. Frederic Burk, addressing a graduation class at Fresno High School:

"We robbed you. We took the bread out of your mouths, you our babes, and fed it to the vultures who were fattening upon our national dishonor. But our sins have been the sins of ignorance rather than of wilfulness. Your fathers were happy, devil-may-care fellows, whose courage, as war patriots, you must in justice honor, but who never had any comprehension of the meaning of a civil patriot nor the slightest realization that it required any of the qualities of courage, self-sacrifice for the common good, and intelligence which in war patriotism we have exemplified."

The book is packed with high-minded fire. It is in the fullest sense a moral tract, fearless and unyielding, certain of its purpose. We don't have anything like it today because the interests—timber, oil, electric power, land development, trucking, railroads, automotive, and all the others which batten on the land today at the expense of tomorrow—are too powerful, at least they are believed too powerful.

But the swing back to serious concern for the environment has begun. Where fifty and sixty years ago the conservationists were concerned about the national parks and the wealth-producing resources—oil, timber, water and minerals—today's movement is concerned of necessity with the total environment. The two movements are motivated by the same basic concern, that is, enhancement of the quality of life, not only for today but for the generations to come.

So I close this catchall of complaint and hope with words of the good Mr. Hyatt for the schoolteachers of his time. Although his language is quaint, the message is as urgent today as it was then.

"A personal appeal is made to the California School Teacher, to take this little manual and use it to the future good of the State you serve. Read it. Surely something in its varied music will strike a responsive chord in you that will vibrate long enough to affect in turn some of the young people with whom you labor, the young people who will so soon be the old people, the young people who so soon will have the destiny of the Golden State in their hands to do with as they may.

"Read it. Try to find at least one idea that is worth passing on. Then, pass it on.

"And may the Future rise up and call you blessed. May it enshrine you in memory as One who would gladly learn and gladly teach."

ILLUSTRATION CREDITS

Aero Photographers: Page 112 bottom right, 115, 117, 118, 134, 135 bottom, 136, 137, 140 top, 141 bottom, 142 bottom, 145, 158, 159, 160, 161 top, 176 top, 181

Air Pollution Research Center, University of California, Riverside: Page 21

Donald Aitken: Page 135 top

Rodney J. Arkley: Page 146, 147

George Ballis: Page 67 bottom, 96 center, 213

Courtesy of the Bancroft Library, University of California, Berkeley: Page 20, 132 bottom

Robert Bastian, San Francisco *Chronicle:* Page 107

Bay Area Air Pollution Control District: Page 17, 23 top

Ed Brady: Page 119 bottom, 141 top, 161 bottom, 180

William Bronson: Frontis, 19, 22 top, 24 bottom, 25, 33 center, 34, 40, 41, 43, 44, 45 top, 47, 48, 51 top and center, 52 top, 53 top and center, 55 top, 56 top, 57 top, 58 bottom, 60 top and center, 63, 64, 67 top, 68 left, 69, 71 center and bottom, 72, 73, 80 bottom, 81 top, 82 top and center, 84, 88 top, 94, 95 bottom, 97 bottom, 98, 99, 101, 103 bottom, 111 top, 113, 119 top and center, 120, 123, 124 top and center, 125 top, 126, 138, 142 top, 155 top, 162, 163 center and bottom, 164, 165, 184 top left and bottom, 185 bottom, 188–189, 194, 195, 196 top, 197, 201, 214 top right and bottom, 215

David Brower: Page 22 bottom, 143

Michael E. Bry: Page 23 bottom, 56–57 bottom, 62 top, 65, 85 bottom, 86, 91, 103 top, 111 bottom, 112 top and bottom left, 114 top, 116 bottom, 125 bottom

California Roadside Council photographs by Pirkle Jones: Page 42 bottom, 46, 49, 50, 51 bottom, 54 center

California State Division of Highways: Page 93, 157 bottom

California State Library: Page 54 top, 132 bottom, 133 top, 148, 156

Paul Chaumont: Page 33 bottom, 58 top and center, 61 top, 62 bottom, 83 top, 88 bottom, 140 bottom

Ray Dunham, California State Department of Fish and Game: Page 27, 28 bottom, 29, 30, 32, 196 bottom, 199 top, 200 bottom

Forestry Library, University of California: Page 211 center

William A. Garnett: Page 151

Philip Hyde: Page 201, 202, 210

Steven M. Johnson: Page 33 top, 125 center

Courtesy KRON-TV San Francisco: Page 66

Kaiser Aluminum News: Page 116 top

Library of Congress: Page 133 bottom

Martin Litton: Page 70

Los Angeles County Air Pollution Control District: Page 18

Los Angeles Times: Page 157 top